the road to Mexico

The Southwest Center Series

Ignaz Pfefferkorn, *Sonora: A Description of the Province*

Carl Lumholtz, *New Trails in Mexico*

Buford Pickens, *The Missions of Northern Sonora: A 1935 Field Documentation*

Gary Paul Nabhan, editor, *Counting Sheep: Twenty Ways of Seeing Desert Bighorn*

Eileen Oktavec, *Answered Prayers: Miracles and Milagros along the Border*

Curtis M. Hinsley and David R. Wilcox, editors, *Frank Hamilton Cushing and the Hemenway Southwestern Archaeological Expedition, 1886–1889,* volume 1: *The Southwest in the American Imagination: The Writings of Sylvester Baxter, 1881–1889*

Lawrence J. Taylor and Maeve Hickey, *The Road to Mexico*

the road to Mexico

text by Lawrence J. Taylor   photographs by Maeve Hickey

The University of Arizona Press   Tucson

Publication of this book is made possible in part
by the proceeds of a permanent endowment
created with the assistance of a Challenge Grant
from the National Endowment for the
Humanities, a federal agency.

The University of Arizona Press
Copyright © 1997
The Arizona Board of Regents
◎ This book is printed on acid-free, archival-quality
paper.
Manufactured in the United States of America
02 01 00 99 98   6 5 4 3 2

Library of Congress Cataloging-in-Publication Data
will be found at the end of this book.

British Library Cataloguing-in-Publication Data
A catalogue record for this book is available from
the British Library.

Frontispiece: Cow-skull building, Amado, Arizona

for our parents,

Virginia and Philip Hickey

and

Harriet and Benjamin Taylor,

and for Daria

And this was really the way my whole road experience began, and the things that were to come are too fantastic not to tell.

Jack Kerouac, *On the Road*

The shape of the road is the road. There is not some other road that wears that shape but only the one.

Cormac McCarthy, *The Crossing*

contents

List of Illustrations   xiii

Preface   xvii

El Mariachi   1

Filling in the Spaces   13

The Mission   29

Jimmy's Diner   39

The Edge of the Res   47

Delia   57

The Three Mikes   63

Green Valleys   77

Ranches and Relics   85

Crossing   101

Mi Nueva Casa   121

Art and Quesadillas   131

La Fiesta de San Francisco   143

Magdalena Off-Season   157

Lost Pilgrims   167

illustrations

Cow-skull building, Amado, Arizona *frontispiece*

Southern Arizona and Northern Sonora xv

Flirting at the fiesta, Santa Ana, Sonora xx

Young performers at the folkloric mass, St. Augustine's Cathedral,
Tucson xxiv

A bride entering St. John the Evangelist Church, Tucson 10

Boys playing on South 6th Avenue, South Tucson 12

San Juan Folklórico at the International Mariachi Conference in Tucson,
1995 25

A detail of a Spanish crucifix at San Xavier del Bac Mission near Tucson
28

A sculpted angel's head on the west wall of San Xavier del Bac Mission
35

Jimmy's Diner on Business 19 (Nogales Highway) near Tucson 38

Giant saguaro near Continental, Arizona 46

An abandoned structure off Old Nogales Highway near Summit,
Arizona 56

A roper's mailbox in Sahuarita, Arizona 62

A contestant waits his turn at a roping, Rio Rico, Arizona   65

By the closed border crossing of Lochiel, Arizona   76

A dancer arranges her coiffure at the Fiesta de Tumacacori   84

Vaqueros on a cigarette break in Arivaca Junction, Arizona   93

Mission wall and bell tower, Tumacacori National Monument   98

Avenida Obregón, Nogales, Sonora   100

A roving musician in Elvira's Restaurant, Nogales, Sonora   109

Father and daughter, Christmas Eve baptism, Nogales, Sonora   110

A thirteen-year-old girl at Mi Nueva Casa, Nogales, Sonora   120

Newly arrived boys at Mi Nueva Casa, Nogales, Sonora   128

Artist Anastacio "Tacho" León, Imuris, Sonora   130

Doña María and her family outside their restaurant, Imuris, Sonora   140

Josécito, an eight-month-old pilgrim, in Magdalena de Kino, Sonora   142

Under a food stand at the Fiesta de San Francisco, Magdalena de Kino   150

O'odham with their saint, Magdalena de Kino   154

A taxi stand in Plaza Juárez, Magdalena de Kino   156

Delivering a statue to a shop, Magdalena de Kino   161

The Day of the Dead in the Magdalena de Kino cemetery   163

A siesta alongside the Río Magdalena   166

Exterior of a home in Las Viguitas near Imuris   170

A home market in Santa Marta, Sonora   175

Pilgrims' robes left at a roadside shrine near Santa Ana   176

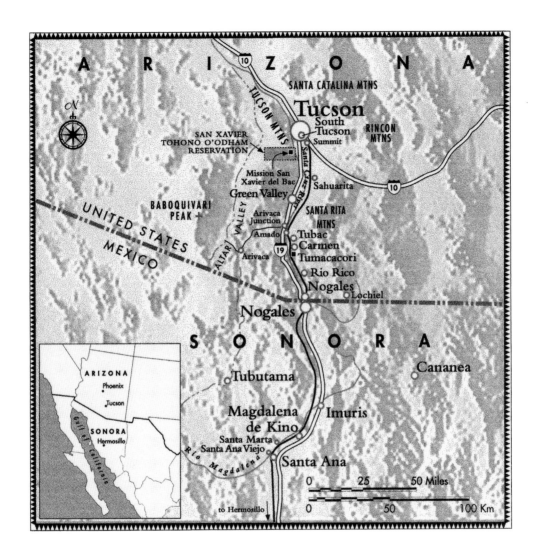

Southern Arizona and northern Sonora

preface

This book had its title long before it was written. *The Road to Mexico* was the name Maeve had given a photograph taken years before of a giant cement cow skull that still sits facing the Cow Palace restaurant in Amado, Arizona, halfway along what had been the main road from Tucson to the Mexican border at Nogales. The skull is actually the facade of a simple rectangular brick building within which a seemingly endless series of commercial aspirations have sputtered.

Pure kitsch, one might have thought. An innocent Americanism, or at best an ironic geste. Yet in the photograph there was something starkly grand, even mysterious, about the skull. Seeing the building itself for the first time, I was not disappointed. Perhaps it was the patina of thirty dusty years, but it seemed an almost natural feature of that burnt landscape, echoing the much larger and only slightly more abstract but natural formation of El Elefante, the massive rock shaped like an elephant's head on the edge of the Santa Rita Mountains, which one could almost always see through the clear desert air across the Santa Cruz valley.

What sort of road provoked such a bestiary? A road that crosses the implacable and yet fragile Sonoran Desert to join Mexico and the United States. A road that began, as colonial roads do, at a point of money and power and penetrated (the metaphor is typically sexual) into "virgin" territory. This road to Mexico began as the road from Mexico, a trail for soldiers and missionaries to the wild edge of New Spain. Ever since that time—and under several flags—a varied and often eccentric lot have been drawn or driven here. They have moved, paused, and settled along it in shifting configurations of race, culture, and identity.

We came here as strangers and, I suppose, pilgrims, like everybody else.

After all, this road has long been a pilgrimage route. Not far west, Baboquivari, the sacred mountain of the native Tohono O'odham, still points a crooked stone finger at the heavens, beckoning its children. And recumbent statues of the early Jesuit missionary to the Far East, San Francisco Xavier, lie here in the Far West, one at a mission just below Tucson and another about 125 miles south in Magdalena de Kino in the Mexican state of Sonora. Between these poles of sacred power, Mexicans, Mexican Americans, Indians, and occasionally others carry their promises, pleas, and thanks. This stream of faithful or hopeful souls swells and diminishes with the seasons, like the desert rivers their road follows.

But there are many others among the truckers, immigrants, drug dealers, retirees, cowboys, tourists, and artists who live and travel along this extraordinary road who might be called pilgrims as well. There is no doubt, at any rate, that Americans—all kinds of Americans—have always sought and found religious experience in more and stranger places than their foreign forebears, in Nature and on the road. Their pilgrimage has always been, not toward the center, but toward the edge, seeking salvation in movement as well as in destination. For Americans the road, like so much else, is about the individual, evoking a free self disconnected from constraints of place: Jack Kerouac and Willie Nelson. But each of us is a latter-day Ulysses, whose journey is also about self-transformation. The restless western pilgrimage has deep roots: a voyage in which one learns to see oneself by moving through places. The question is, Can one also learn to see others, people like those who voyage along this road or have settled on its edge, momentarily or for generations, raising monuments to their passing and their presence? And in making such a journey, can one find Mexico?

We tried, moving like uncertain pilgrims up and down the road. This book is a partial record of our passage. It contains the traces of a series of encounters—amusing, painful, often strange, and nearly always unforeseen. Our pilgrimage, like that of many we met, followed an eccentric itinerary. We set out to learn something about a particular road to Mexico that nature and history have conspired to make unique. Though this book is by no means a comprehensive account of what can be seen along the road. It is a fragmentary view, but there is a particular truth to be found in fragments. Perhaps we have followed the example of some of the people we met in resisting the impulse to connect all the dots.

The book is also the record, as well as the product, of our collaboration, still another aesthetic project facilitated by this road. A photographer and a writer, we traveled the road, met people separately and together, and spoke to one another from time to time about what we were seeing and hearing. The result is two parallel narratives—one in pictures and another in words—that occasionally touch. Photos and text interact with, rather than illustrate, each other. Their dual presence suggests something about the ways in which the world presents itself to, and is represented by, different eyes and voices.

From the very beginning, this project has enjoyed generous financial and intellectual support from Joseph C. Wilder of the University of Arizona's Southwest Center. We want to thank him for his friendship and for his help at every phase of our work. Also unfailing has been the enthusiasm and cogent editorial advice of University of Arizona Press editor Christine Szuter. Some of our work was aided by a grant from Lafayette College, which we gratefully acknowledge here. We also want to give special thanks to Anne Keyl of the University of Arizona Press; Tim Fuller and his assistant, Greg Huston, of Tim Fuller Photography, who did the final print-

Flirting at the fiesta, Santa Ana, Sonora

ing of the photographs; Gregory McNamee for reading the manuscript and making helpful suggestions; and David Yetman of the Southwest Center for his friendship and frequent aid and advice. We were helped in every possible way—from living accommodations to invaluable advice to the personal stories and photographs that are the substance of this book—by dozens of people along the road. Among them, we need to thank especially Robert Barnacastle, Ellen Basso, Judith and Julio Bernal, Victor J. Borg, Edward Encinas, the Felix family, Bernard Fontana, Jim Griffith, the Herod family, Adela Hice, Jane the waitress, Marguerite Jarvis, Anastacio León, Cynthia Lindquist, Doña María, the Martinez family, Melissa McCormick, Gino Molina, Dorothy Muscat, Jean and Dr. William Neubauer, Myrna Ortega, Lisa Otey, Antonio Pazos, Carmen Villa Prezelski, Claudia Proto, Doña Ramona, Barbara Ruppman, Francisco and Anthony Sanchez, Thomas E. Sheridan, M. Jan Smith-Florez, Rosamond Spicer, Roberta "Birdie" Stable, David Tineo, Vivian Turner, Jimmy Veck, Peggy and Elizabeth Wilder, and Kathleen Williamson, and many other people whose names we never knew. We have changed the identity of those who did not wish their names to be used, and we wish to take this opportunity to thank them without jeopardizing their anonymity.

the road to Mexico

Young performers at the folkloric mass, St. Augustine's Cathedral, Tucson

el mariachi

"Lots of cars get stolen down there. Where? Oh, I guess just about anywhere down there, except maybe Rocky Point. Rocky Point is very civilized. There are too many Americans down there for them to be doing much. And if you see a road-block, well, what do you know? Maybe it's the government, but you never know with those people."

This advice was offered, along with maps, by a sensible silver-haired woman in the branch office of the American Automobile Association on Oracle Road near what is for the moment the northern edge of the city.

Tucson is an immense, green and concrete picnic continually spreading across a flat basin, a hundred square miles of grid highways and streets encircled, but not contained, by a range of mountains for each cardinal direction.

To get to the AAA—indeed, to get anywhere in Tucson—one drives past at least three malls and a dozen Circle K convenience stores. Toward the edge of town, the yellow-gray desert reasserts itself, only to be interrupted by the newest cluster of Santa Fe–style patio homes, or a pastel strip mall like that housing the AAA office, a beige-carpeted, climate-controlled world of stacked maps and vacation brochures.

The attendant continued, unfolding the map and marking the suggested route with a thick red line.

"Just take Oracle to Prince and get right on I-10 south, then I-19. I recommend the missions at San Xavier and Tumacacori. The exits are well marked, and they are just off the interstate."

If we felt the understandable urge to dabble in the exotic, to have a drink on the other side and buy what used to be called curios, we could park our car in Nogales, Arizona, and walk across into the swirl of the other Nogales, following the hats and shorts of American tourists as they streamed into Avenida Obregón, with its piles of serapes, heaps of polychromatic clay pots, and persistent hawkers. Buy a piñata, have a Corona, and go back to the United States.

We could in this way avoid both Mexico in Mexico and Mexico in Arizona. And all "those people."

The beginning of any voyage is crucial, defining the line and limit of its path, and the AAA is perhaps not the best place to begin the road to Mexico. What we see first frames what we see later, just as the frame of a painting separates and defines as extraordinary what lies within and—more subtly, through its own color, texture, and design—guides and shapes our expectations. More elusively, each painting we view is framed by others we have seen before. Walking through an exhibit, the ghosts of other canvases hover near the ones on the walls, enhancing and obscuring our view.

In that sense, each image we encounter along the road to Mexico is framed by previous impressions to form a series of paintings—landscapes, portraits, abstract impressions—each framed, even haunted, by older images.

But the art gallery experience may no longer be the most apt. We are all too mediatized. The cinema frame may be a more appropriate image.

We set out on the road to Mexico, to make our own road pictures: mental movies, pre-plotted to some extent. At the very least we are looking for characters, encounters, the fulfillment of expectations, versions of Mexico.

It would be hard to escape all that. Even the desire to foil expectations—to *not* see the Mexico of myth, song, and television commercial—is itself an intention, a focus that blinds one to the stereotype that is in fact sometimes realized.

Just as every Mexican coming north already has a notion of America, which is why he or she is coming, so do Americans have well-developed images of Mexico. The images are constructed in the realm of popular culture, from movies to television commercials to tourist icons. For many, perhaps most, Americans the images remain disconnected: tacos, sombreros, burros, mariachis, Aztec pyramids. Each item is produced to sell something: a lunch, a mood, a vacation.

If any of us bring these images together to form a more coherent set of mental pictures, perhaps a narrative, it is because that story is important. That myth of Mexico has a job to do, defining the Other just across the border, whether man or woman, landscape or townscape, darkly dangerous or warmly embracing, alluringly exotic or repellent, fertility or filth, order or chaos.

There may well be a real personal need involved in this mythmaking. We may be motivated by fear, longing, or, often enough, a mixture of the two.

San Francisco journalist Richard Rodriguez, raised English-speaking and at a certain distance from his father, was driven by the image of his own incongruously dark Indian face to seek his *Days of Obligation* across the border. For Rodriguez the most intimate aspect of his person—the face as self—is reflected back to him in the looking glass of American culture, refracted as well as reflected, into what is salient here: race. Embracing the logic of opposition, he entered Mexico looking for the Other within, the dark Catholic below the border.

He could find only what he was looking for, just as the white supremacist who fearfully watches the border for the flow of "mud people" is in no danger of being disappointed.

All ambiguity is unsettling—for it is not only Mexico that is at stake, it is America. It is not only they who, if allowed, might resist the confinement of mythology. We too might surprise ourselves.

The photographer Dorothea Lange, in describing her method of capturing the life of a California Dust Bowl camp, put it this way: "Every day you must go out and forget what you know, forget what you've seen the day before." An impossible mission, but a bracing corrective, perhaps, for the natural human tendency to do just the opposite: to remember, and thus to subjugate the new to the old. It is a way of looking at the world that allows the thing that does not fit to show itself.

We must go to Mexico, but we must watch where we are going.

I-19 thrusts the traveler out of Tucson and directly into a generalized America in which even the most distinctive landscape becomes merely a backdrop. But the interstate subordinates the distinctive humanscape as well, gliding over the predominantly poor and Mexican western edge of Tucson. Like the information highway, it is reductive and seductive in its slick, expansive trajectory. The gaze, by virtue of the speed, is never intimate; it can only fix on the grand vista and the occasional imposing punctuation. You float south, raised serenely above tawdry eccentricities, at once generic and local, ranged along the Nogales and Old Nogales Highways. Those roads offer a different route to Mexico. It began for us on a Sunday morning after the mariachi mass at Saint Augustine's Cathedral in what is left of downtown Tucson.

This is El Centro, though its Mexican character may not be immediately apparent. Rolling along Broadway on a June afternoon, it is 107 degrees, and the only people out of their cars are bone-thin, sun-blasted Anglo freaks, their dust-encrusted yellow beards pointing in all directions. They make their apparently pointless way across parking lots or down median strips. As in most western cities, you can find the downtown by heading toward the office towers visible for miles in every direction. These monoliths of glass and concrete dropped several decades ago from corporate and government heaven. A process called, strangely, urban renewal swept away dozens of old adobe homes, entire barrios.

Some remain, however, like Barrio Viejo, below Cushing Street, where rows of pastel yellow, ocher, and blue adobe homes still cluster around the Chinese market and the fabulously ornate, now padlocked, Teatro Carmen. Or tiny Barrio Anita—a couple of dozen old adobe and frame houses tucked into a sandy pocket between the railroad and the highway. Barrio Anita, with its vibrant murals and the Anita Street Market, whose homemade tortillas and green-corn tamales may be the best in Tucson.

For the people of these and other Mexican neighborhoods, the cathedral still provides one of the principal stages on which to perform their life passages, from baptisms to funerals, and has a mariachi mass every Sunday morning at eight.

We arrived just in time to squeeze into the remaining space on the side of the church nearest the band. The men in the congregation were dressed casually in the southwestern fashion, but the women—especially the young women—were brightly, alluringly wrapped. And nearly every infant girl or toddler was a real showpiece, her outfit assembled like a wedding cake with layers of stiffened lace trim on white stockings above gleaming patent leather shoes, balanced by equally fanciful headpieces: ribbons, bands, and hats trimmed, turned, and twisted into eye-catching sculptures.

The mass was in Spanish, and the music that morning was provided by Tierra del Sol. The men, bellies swelling against their bright-buttoned outfits, play here in church as they do elsewhere, with an easy elegance, passing the lead from one to another, now guitar, now violin, now trumpet. The two young women who had joined their ranks were, if anything, even more confident: brazenly bowing the violins as if female mariachi were not a recent innovation. Their religious repertoire seemed little different from their secular one, though there were none of the whoops with which mariachi music can be punctuated. Even so, the musicians were as relaxed and happy as ever—nodding, smiling, and chatting with one another throughout, strolling forward for string solos as the happy staccato of the trumpets propelled the piece along.

We followed the crowd out into the vestibule after the mass, where a number of women asked for and received healing prayers from the visiting Franciscan abbot. But most of the congregation, chatting amiably in Spanish and English, poured out into the sun-washed morning and made their way next door to the community hall, where the women of the Altar Society were busily ladling steaming menudo (a soup of intestines served only and always on weekend mornings) with pride and flare into cardboard bowls and rolling breakfast burritos of beans, machaca (dried and reconstituted beef), potatoes, and spicy chorizo sausage. Most of the long tables were already full of families and groups of friends, and, feeling shy about intruding on such a Sunday morning ritual, we headed to the only empty corner.

Within moments we were no longer alone. One of the mariachis, a fortyish horn player, along with his diminutive mother, took seats near us and nodded a greeting. We told him how much we enjoyed the music, and he told us something of his love for the art. The conversation resumed days later in his apartment.

"It was all started by an Irish priest named Father O'Rourke in 1963," Fernando told us. "There were a couple of groups playing some mariachi before then, but he's the one who really got it going. He was a jazz pianist and he loved mariachi, so he got together with Father Carillo. That was a goal of theirs, to start a mariachi in the church. The first one was in All Saints, just a few blocks from here."

We were sitting on the sofa in Fernando's temporary quarters, an immaculately ordered apartment just south of Broadway, very near the cathedral and close to every home he has ever lived in. The apartment is small, and Fernando shares it with a teenaged son and daughter. Anthony was a handsome teenager with a hint of the look and speech of the tough downtown schools, but his every gesture was marked by an easy grace and the courtliness that seems part of the style of the mariachi. He was clearly a fanatic like his father. Fernando's daughter, Jessica, a very pretty, round-faced sixteen-year-old, sat in the open kitchen a few yards away, poring over her homework and looking up to smile silently when the conversation interested her.

There were no visible signs of Mexico, and in fact decoration of any kind was spare. But the music filled that void. Across the narrow room from our sofa was a wall of turntables, tuners, and speakers, and by the time we had finished our greetings Anthony had popped in a cassette called *Mariachi Vargas Plays the Classics*. Horns blared arias from *Carmen* as we continued our discussion of mariachi in Tucson and in the lives of Fernando and Anthony Sanchez.

"I got into mariachi music basically because my mom and dad wanted me to play the trumpet. That's because I was born with asthma. They wanted me to play mariachi music, to play trumpet and build up my lungs. You are influenced by your parents at that age, and I wanted to sound like Herb Alpert, basically," he said, laughing.

"He was my idol. But then I heard Fuentes of Mariachi Vargas and I said, 'That sounds good too. I want to sound like that.' I started at fifteen. I'll be forty in February, so I've been playing mariachi music for twenty-five years. I've had my diversions. I was into Latin rock music. I'm still a very big rock fan, but I play mariachi. I played for years with a group called Los Changuitos. I've been with La Tierra del Sol for three years now. We're all career people. I'm a banker by trade. The leader of the group is with the Alumni Association over at the University of Arizona. He runs the group, and another member is an engineer. He used to play with me when I was with the Changuitos.

"I guess the music really took off, and Tucson became the capital of mariachi music in the United States since the convention started in 1983. It's really been great financially, bringing lots of money into the city. But there's a cultural side, to show the kids there is something besides gangs. The kids who play the music, they have their outlets." His eyes included his son.

"Is it working?" I asked. "Are many young people interested in mariachi and does it keep them out of gangs?"

"I can't say that it's working. It's getting worse and worse. . . . We had gangs too, but back then if you had a problem with someone, you would settle it with your fists, maybe throw rocks, but not with guns." Rediscovering his hope, he added: "But if it means keeping one kid out of a gang, it's worth it."

The music was a bond between these two men, who might otherwise have drifted apart, separated by the enclosing realities of their respective worlds: Fernando in the bank, Anthony on the street. The father seemingly had discovered an equilibrium, working hard to pursue a career in the day and giving his evenings to music. But the son seemed troubled by a dissonance in his world.

"None of my friends are into mariachi. One of my friends even disrespects it, disrespects Mexican things. Like, he takes on more black things, you know? I think the culture is important, like the whites, the blacks, and us, we've all got our cultures."

His father continued: "But to me the music means so much more than that. It comes from the soul. It's a sort of poetry. It's an art, definitely an art."

Meanwhile, Anthony too had been thinking about the meaning of mariachi. "Sometimes we play for older ladies and grandmothers, like a present from their daughters and granddaughters. They get all emotional when we play for them." His face was pure satisfaction.

Fernando nodded in agreement. "We played at an old folks home. It really choked me up to see the way the music moved them, what it meant to them. To be honest," he laughed, "we didn't really sound that good, but to them we sounded like the Vargas or something like that!" They both laughed, enjoying the self-deprecation almost as much as the memory of the pleasure they had brought to the old people.

Fernando went on to discuss the musical character of mariachi, which he saw as the queen of Mexican music, containing within it all the others.

"Mariachi is a symbol. It is all of Mexico."

But what about that part of Mexico just down the road?

"I've never been past Nogales. All that tourist junk, and the filth and poverty. I figure it's like that all along the border. You'd have to go a hundred miles south to get beyond that." His face contorted with the bad taste in his mouth.

I protested, but he would have none of it. Fernando was not about to risk the Mexico of his imagination, of his mariachi, by penetrating that border. He would consider flying over it, landing in the center of the nation, in the Guadalajara of Mariachi Vargas, but Fernando Sanchez was not going to take the road to Mexico.

We did. But not before hearing Fernando perform again, for two weddings in the cathedral. The first had a vaquero theme. The groom and his party wore gleaming cowboy boots and mariachi suits: tight pants, white shirts, ribbon ties, and bolero jackets tricked out with boutonnieres of rope hanging with gold charms of horses, saddles, horseshoes, and bulls. The bride and her bridesmaids floated in on clouds of chiffon to the strains of the mariachi. Their wrist corsages and bouquets were of ribbons and flowers but glittered with the same vaquero charms. A little boy strode proudly up to the altar bearing a white straw cowboy hat festooned with more cowboy symbols and the wedding rings, dangling from ribbons. One of the bridesmaids, we were told, had designed it all. Joyous and buoyant as the occasion was, the young couple were solemn and dignified throughout. They betrayed no surprise at finding themselves starring in such a pageant, posing frequently for the flashing cameras with a practiced and perfect poise, like the bride and groom

A bride entering St. John the Evangelist Church, Tucson

atop a Mexican wedding cake. "A fairy tale wedding," as one guest remarked.

A darker story was enacted on the same stage some days later. Though a wedding had been announced in the church bulletin for that hour, the cathedral was cavernously empty at seven on a Friday evening. We were about to leave when the doors finally swung open and two middle-aged women appeared, followed by the bride in an elegant and unusually restrained ivory dress.

They appeared mysteriously stricken, as if they had just heard the news of some mortal accident. For a long while there were only the three of them—bride, mother, and mother's sister. Not another soul could be seen either inside the church or in the foyer, where there should have been crowds of parading adults and darting children.

The women stood there, nearly silent, arranging the bride's gown with great care for the walk up the aisle. But there was no one there to escort her. Finally, an older man who seemed to be her father appeared in the front row, equally elegant and leaning weakly on an elaborately carved, gold-handled cane. He was followed by the handsome and immaculate young groom. No other guests arrived. The silence and emptiness were leaden, and all the participants stood as if under the weight of unbearable tragedy.

Suddenly there was a burst of trumpets (the mariachis had quietly entered by the side), and the main door swung open for the aunt, the matron of honor, solemn and perfect in her traditional slow march down the aisle. As the bride followed, alone, her mother faced her from the front of the church, gesturing directions: Hold up your bouquet, slow down. Absolute decorum was preserved throughout, with every detail correct, all on a grand stage with no audience but us. As the couple joined hands at the altar, the bride's father began to sob quietly while his wife patted him in consolation.

The musicians began again, singing now with gusto, as though to a full cathedral. The music echoed in the emptiness.

Boys playing on South 6th Avenue, South Tucson

filling in the spaces

Stone Avenue, having passed the cathedral, the Mexican consulate, an old syna-
gogue, and a black Baptist church, joins South Sixth Avenue. This is the main drag
of South Tucson, a separate and largely Mexican American city. Some old adobe
homes sit on parched lots to the west at the edge of a brushy desert that rises into
the Tucson Mountains, but most people live in the hundreds of very modest tract
houses lining quiet side streets.

South Sixth Avenue and the other broad avenues that run north–south are, by
contrast, jumping with life. After midnight, young people bump, roar, and screech
their low riders up and down the avenues, pausing at the drive-up windows of
package stores to buy six-packs through heavy iron bars. But even in the blasting
sun of a summer afternoon Sixth Avenue is a bursting whirl of bail-bond dealers,
thrift shops, family-run Mexican restaurants competing with fast-food chains, and
pastel pink and turquoise shops offering piñatas or religious artifacts. Mexico ab-
hors a vacuum, and nearly every sandy field or parking lot is occupied by a mobile
taquería offering the cuisine of Sonora, Sinaloa, or Jalisco.

The walls—cement, brick, plaster—are adorned with graffiti or murals. We
found one at Tenth Avenue and Twenty-seventh Street, where a vibrant panorama

of Mexican gods and warriors encircles a more mundane power source: the South Tucson electric generating station. This is disputed territory, a no-man's-land between Yaqui Indian and Chicano neighborhoods. When the walls were blank, rival gangs "tagged" them in the angry fugue of graffiti, and the power company painted them over every Monday. Finally someone suggested that a mural might end the cycle and asked Antonio Pazos to take on the project.

I met Antonio at the El Rio Community Center—a group of bustling offices, classrooms, and open spaces just beyond the dry bed of the Santa Cruz River on the western edge of the city. Like Antonio's mural, the Center forms a kind of border among neighborhoods, but in this case the neighborhoods are five barrios that are often at war. Nothing going on inside hinted at such hostilities, however. Smiling workers assisted a steady stream of people, helping them fill out forms, handing out lunch baskets, advising, and joking about the vicissitudes of local life.

Antonio, the assistant director of the Center, is a tall, darkly handsome Sonoran with a self-assured smile and always lively eyes. He told me how, twenty years before, he came to begin Tucson's mural "movement" more or less by accident.

"I had just graduated from Arizona State University and was on my way home to Hermosillo when some friends here at the Center asked me if I knew how to paint murals. They had money and a wall, and I said yes. I was picturing something the size of a door maybe. Then they showed me the wall out there!" He pointed out the window to a very large and gaily decorated expanse of stucco. "And I said, 'Oh shit.' It was huge!"

Apparently, Antonio's total immersion baptism in mural painting went well enough. He successfully completed that mural and began teaching his art at Pima Community College, helping to form the next generation of Tucson muralists. He's still teaching, as is at least one of his early students, David Tineo of Barrio Anita, whose work is visible all over Tucson.

"Now there are a great deal of good vibes," Antonio continued, "but in the early days it wasn't easy. There was a lot of resistance and criticism, particularly from academics—art professors. They called it propaganda art. There were lots of bad reviews. And there was no money. You were lucky if somebody gave you two or three hundred bucks for the paint. But slowly things got better. The murals got better, and educated people started thinking that we were a bona fide movement. Little by little, small grants came in, and a real important moment was the exhibit at the Tucson Museum of Art in 1989—the Cara Show—that showed the history of the mural art movement in California, New Mexico, and Arizona. David Tineo and I did the mural on the outside of the museum. Justice was done when they invited us to do that. The movement was accepted."

Now there are about two hundred murals brightening walls all over Tucson, especially in the more or less continuous band of barrios stretching along the western and southern edges of the city, from Old Pasqua—settled by Yaqui Indians seeking asylum from Mexico early in the century—through the El Rio district, Barrio Anita, and the other downtown barrios, and then down into South Tucson and beyond. Into this world muralists bring art whose effects they understand in practical terms. Murals are, for them, not so much products as processes in which the barrio youth become active collaborators.

"In my own work the imagery has evolved. I did have some experience with murals before coming here, in California. I was there in 1972 helping the farm-workers. We also went around to the camps on flatbed trucks to give concerts and plays, trying to use art in a social movement, to unify the farm workers and support them. Coming here, the issues were different—bilingual education, police brutality, and of course the immigration issue. And racism is back in vogue, but more sophisticated and subtle. There are different cultural problems here, less identity."

I told Antonio that I had already met Chicanos who seemed to fear Mexico and who were reluctant to go there. He looked pained.

"People have to go there with an open mind. It's like any foreign country. It's not going to be the same as the United States. And people are so quick to judge when they travel. If something isn't just exactly what they're used to, they complain bitterly and say they're never going back. That really hurts. The Chicanos from here, they can be as bad as anyone that way. And there's another thing; many of them are embarrassed to go to Mexico because of their language. A Mexican will go up to a Chicano, and if he is brown, if he looks like me, of course the Mexican will speak Spanish to him, and if the Chicano doesn't speak it like a native, the Mexican will be disgusted. He'll say, 'Look at you, you're brown. How come you can't speak Spanish?' or, 'You have the prickly pear in your face.' So they have a self-esteem problem, and that also affects their attitude toward Mexico.

"I see the murals as a way I can help to educate the kids about where they come from, and to help their self-esteem by knowing who and what they are. These people are pretty poor. Many don't own much. They don't have the cars and homes they see on TV. But they have their dignity and their past and traditions. I tell them that the dominant society may have everything else, but they don't have our strong identity, history, and heritage. When they try to take away who we are, our culture, it makes us angry."

Antonio seemed to be speaking more for himself than anyone else, but he wanted to give a cultural shape to the often inchoate anger of the barrio youth.

"I want to teach them that they have these rich possessions even if they don't know them, don't know their own history. The murals show them that there were gods looking after us years ago."

A few days later, Antonio met me at the power station mural. Standing there in the quiet afternoon, he explained the surrounding social scene.

"It's about territory. Mainstream America may think that it's about pride, but it's not that. What happens is that the drug dealers in this town have been smart enough to divide their territories into marketing districts. This is about business.

"Now, usually the capo—the head honcho of the gang—is the one to have the connections with the drug dealer, who'll give him money and weapons, and finance special projects for the gang. And he is in charge of making sure that everybody thinks it's about neighborhood and pride, 'You see the southsiders, you kick their ass. Kill them if you have to.' The head honcho has lieutenants and soldiers, and if anyone gets out of line, he gets punished—I've seen it at the center—so those kids, even the lieutenants and other soldiers, get fooled into thinking that it's about pride.

"In this town there are the Bloods, based in L.A.—it's a black gang—and Crips, who are out of Arizona, Texas, and New Mexico. They were created in prisons. And now there is another faction, the Mexican Mafia, that controls the west side, El Rio, Barrio Hollywood. They are also organized from prisons here, with dealers coming up from Nogales, San Luis, Agua Prieta—all the border towns. So most of the city is divided up between these three factions, but within each one there are still hostile local groups controlling drugs in their own 'marketing district,' and Crips will kill Crips because of a bad deal or something that went down in prison. It's about money. That's the way it is, whether we like it or not."

Nevertheless, for Antonio the murals had the power not only to represent but also to recreate and re-narrate that world. Here, graffiti had given way to brilliant purple, yellow, red, and green figures: Yaqui deer dancers, Aztec warriors and gods, conquistadors and Virgins. In telling their story of Mexico there on South Tenth Avenue, these figures—shimmering in the desert sun—seemed to claim that the surrounding houses squatting on bleak, sandy lots were home to their still-heroic descendants, whose lives were but a difficult chapter in a continuing saga.

"How do you get the kids in the neighborhood to help you with the murals?" we asked Antonio.

"It's easy," he replied. "I just start painting, and pretty soon somebody shows up and threatens me. 'Hey, what the fuck do you think you're doin' there, that's our wall.' ''Bout time you showed up,' I say. 'This is your mural, and we've got a lotta work to do."

In this case he had begun with a panel dedicated to the Yaqui Indians. "I'm from near Hermosillo and we all have some Yaqui blood," Antonio told me.

There are still Yaquis in that part of Sonora, but many had been killed or driven out by the Mexican government early in the century, and a large number had sought asylum here in Arizona. By the curious logic of U.S. categories, it took these people until just a few years ago to receive official tribal status and a small reservation—New Pasqua—in the desert southwest of Tucson. Most of their history in Arizona has been urban. They settled in a few westside barrios. Some have remained more Yaqui than others who, to varying degrees, have merged into the Chicano population. For the self-consciously Yaqui, language and religion are central, with religion spanning a syncretic range of rites and beliefs that merge traditional forms with Catholic crosses and a splendid Easter ceremony. One of the remaining Yaqui neighborhoods is located at the southern edge of South Tucson, ten blocks from the mural. Several dozen of the poorest houses in the area cluster around a large sandlot where battered pickups bump through the dust or park before an open-front chapel dedicated to Saint Martin de Porres but home to dozens of saints and religious images.

Starting on the end of the power company wall that was closest to their territory, Antonio had begun his Yaqui wall with the most ubiquitous of cultural symbols: the deer dancer.

I had already seen several performances and many pictures. The dancer is always clad in skins, his ankles wound with bands of cocoon rattles. On his cloth-swathed head sits an antlered deer's head. Bent forward with down-stretched arms, the dancer punctuates the slow-stepping, whirring rattle of his ankles with shakes of hand-held gourds. If the dance is well done, and if you know how to watch it, the expressionless human face disappears and the deer becomes ethereally real.

Here on the wall, however, the dancer proved a contentious figure. It was queried first by hostile Chicanos, who had no trouble recognizing an enemy 'flag,' as Anthony explained.

" 'Hey, how come the Indian stuff, man. That's *our* fuckin' wall!' he reminded me. Yeah, they were pissed, but I whipped out my drawings — showing my design for the whole mural and the story of Mexico that it would tell. 'You have your part too,' I told them, and from there on it went pretty smooth. They organized themselves into groups to paint."

But not all the Yaquis were happy with the picture, either. They can be understandably ambivalent about Mexico's appropriation of their deer dancer — as part of the state seal of Sonora, for example — even though few groups of Mexico's Indians have fared worse in recent times.

Antonio's claim of Yaqui ancestry may or may not have been accepted, but at least one Yaqui queried his rendition of the dancer.

"He said to me, 'Man, as many deer dancers as I have seen in my life, I never saw one with his leg raised up high like this.' He was right. They don't raise a leg that high, but I explained to him that I wanted it like that for the composition, it was more powerful like that. With his leg up, he looks like he's is coming forward, out of the painting." The design remained.

The rest of the mural depicts Antonio's conception of the history of Mexico. In the first section, the three ships of Christopher Columbus near the shores of the New World, their billowing sails emblazoned with skulls and crossbones. I asked why.

"We are a mestizo race, a mixed race. Most Mexicans are half Spanish and half Indian. I wanted to show the beginning of that phenomenon. The ships came from

Spain. But with pirate symbols, because that's truly how I view their invasion. If it had been an exchange, . . . but they subjugated the Mexicans. They fooled them and tricked them big time. We have a totally different concept of civilization and idiosyncratic ideas. They took advantage of us, and they figured that we were stupider than they were. All the disease they brought, the violence and ignorance. The cultures here in Mesoamerica were very advanced, and the Spanish came here with their new god," he laughed, "and they messed everything up."

It was not just Antonio's varying point of reference, in which "Mexicans" were alternately the original Indians or mestizos but never Spanish, that bespoke an ambivalence, if not a confusion, about the identity of Mexicans in general and this Mexican in particular. Antonio's mood seemed to shift as he spoke, with anger, intellectual curiosity, wonder, and mild irony each playing a part in his view of Mexico's history and his own.

Nor is the mural single-minded, for if the Spanish arrived as pirates, the meeting of Cortez and Montezuma—the subject of the next section—did not hint at any future betrayal. They are shown as equally noble, bowing to one another.

Smiling broadly at the scene, Antonio remarked: "Two different ways of thinking. I would give anything to have been there, to have watched when Cortez and Montezuma met." It was as if he were speculating on his own conception.

Behind the two leaders loom huge female forms, confronting each other like the much smaller heroes beneath them. Antonio explained that the figure behind Cortez represents the famous seventeenth-century apparition of the Virgin to the poor Indian Juan Diego, an event that would turn what had been a relatively minor Spanish incarnation of Mary into the focus of the world's largest Catholic pilgrimage.

"I have the Virgin of Guadalupe because I wanted once and for all to make a definite statement about what I think about Guadalupe and how she was used to colonize the Indians. What happened is this. When Guadalupe appeared to the Indian, she spoke in Nahuatl, and everyone figured, because she spoke Nahuatl and looked Indian, that she had to be Tonantzin. Juan Diego himself thought that it was Tonantzin."

That Aztec goddess is pictured in the mural near a pyramid, behind Montezuma. She is shown much like Guadalupe, tall and holding a long cloth with stars but wearing a splendid headdress radiating feathers of green, yellow, and red.

"She was the goddess of the humble and the poor, and whenever the poor had a necessity, she would help them. So naturally Juan Diego thought, 'She speaks Nahuatl, she looks Indian, how could she be Spanish?' But when he went to tell the bishop, the bishop said, 'Well, that's Guadalupe.' The Church figured they'd fool the Indians by saying it was Guadalupe, and the Indians thought, 'We'll make them believe we think it's Guadalupe, but we know it's Tonantzin.'"

Antonio smiled mischievously at what he viewed as a clever subversion. Whether the deception was contrived or a less conscious episode in the evolution of popular religion, I thought something like that had probably happened. But if so, I was equally sure that the rereading of images, the borrowing of gods for local purposes, had not ended and would never end. Did Tonantzin and the other Aztec gods in the mural mean the same for the barrio kids as they did for Antonio? I thought that for the locals they probably only figured as generic emblems of Aztec culture, itself a symbol of a Mexican culture under construction. Guadalupe, on the other hand, was a real person, imprinted on their walls and in their hearts. Yet, the Mexican Guadalupe may still be Tonantzin, and maybe her children still recognize her as such even if they have forgotten her name. Perhaps that was Antonio's point.

Beyond Tonantzin there are other Aztec deities on the wall: Quetzalcoatl the plumed serpent, a diving eagle god clutching a snake in his talons, and the star-maker, a pale, floating Aztec statue with a shower of stars floating up from a basket on his back and arching over his head and across the night sky. The artist spoke of every detail with unrestrained enthusiasm, more interested in the imagery than the technique.

Around the corner is the rest of Mexican history—epitomized in the floating portraits of four heroes: Father Hidalgo, Juárez, and the revolutionary heroes Zapata and Pancho Villa. That last panel had come from an unusual source, as Antonio explained.

"All the time we were painting here, the people in the house there across the street were very friendly, very nice. They gave us lemonade while we worked. One day the man there, Miguel, told me a story about a friend he had in prison years ago. When the friend died he had one precious thing, and he left it to Miguel— a tablecloth on which he had carefully drawn the four makers of modern Mexico. Miguel showed me the drawing, and I asked him would he like me to use that design for a mural. That's why I added his friend's name there at the bottom: R. Mendez, R.I.P." A history lesson for Antonio, for Miguel the wall was a memorial to a prison friendship.

This mural, like many others, has mainly resisted graffiti, but some 'tagging' had found the deer dancer—evidence, perhaps, of the small and dwindling number of Yaquis compared to the Chicano population of the area. Where Antonio had painted "stop the violence," someone had written 'start,' but someone else had nearly effaced the emendation. Another alteration still stood, the paint still fresh: "Barrios Unidos" (United Barrios) had been changed to read "Barrio Libre," a traditional name for the Chicano neighborhood just to the north.

1995 was a banner year for homicides in Tucson and the surrounding area: ninety-four in a population of 666,880 for Pima County. Within Tucson and South Tucson these deaths were very much concentrated in the barrios, and about half of all homicides for which the cause was known were drug related. All this was publicized in a special January 7, 1996, Sunday supplement in the *Arizona Daily Star*. There was also a map of Tucson showing the concentration of deaths along the corridor of westside and southside barrios.

That surprised no one, but all those numbers clustered in their own neighborhoods and not in others had impressed a group of teenagers I met working on another mural on the west side of town. When I met them a week later, they were talking about the supplement, in which they and their project were also featured. A photo of their sweet-faced fifteen-year-old friend, Peter Valenzuela of Barrio Anita, had been among the fifty portraits of the slain included in the feature.

Julio, a muralist in his fifties, was helping the team of young artists who worked on and under a scaffold, filling in the details of leaves, belts, and petals. His wife, Judith, told me the story of Peter's death and of the response: this mural, entitled *Por Vida* (For Life).

"He was at the movies down on Valencia with his sister and friends. They were waiting for a ride, but it was late, so they decided to walk home, up Tenth Avenue. A car went by with some B-12 kids in it. They're Bloods. The driver did a U-turn and drove back, and another kid leaned out the window and yelled at them and shot Peter in the face, killing him.

"There is nothing for these kids, no counseling or therapy, and they have to deal with this kind of thing all the time. And the police, who are afraid to deal with the real gangs—the Bloods and Crips—hassle all these kids constantly. I'm not saying they're angels. They're not. They'll do beer runs and things like that. But they are not the big pushers, and they are not murderers. Anyway, the mural gives them some way of handling it, of dealing with their pain and anger. We are anxious that they do that rather than look for revenge."

The plan for the mural includes a central portrait of two very young looking parents joined lovingly over an infant, all of them in the encircling, protective embrace of the Virgin of Guadalupe. Below is a heap of roses, and on either side are the standard emblems of Indian culture: the Yaqui deer dancer and the Aztec warrior. The design for the warrior came out of a book, but the deer dancer was drawn from life by Gino Molina.

"I am part Yaqui," Gino told me, "from Barrio Anita, but I go down to the Pasqua a lot to watch the ceremonies. My primo [cousin] is studying to be a deer dancer."

The plan also includes portraits of four recently slain youths from nearby barrios and a list of thirty-five names of barrio dead from all over the city.

The kids continued to work on the mural, leaning into an Aztec warrior god's costume to the blaring sounds of gangsta rap. Pausing for a snack of Taco Bell tacos, two of the young artists, Jessie and Jesus, returned to the subject of the newspaper article.

"The way I see it," Jesus said, "next year things will quiet down a little. Then it [the murder rate] will go up again. Like, '98 is going to be a big year, a deadly year."

"Yeah," Jessie agreed, "because I had a dream, man. It scared the shit out of me. I saw a tombstone that had a name on it, and the dates 1979 to 1998. Like, I knew it was my name, dude, but I wouldn't look at it. Shit, man, that scared the shit out of me."

It is a common Mexican practice to mark the spot of a death, particularly on the road, with a cross or a more elaborate marker. The site sometimes grows into a full-fledged shrine, adorned by visitors with flowers, messages, or other mementos of the deceased or of the occasions and holidays since his or her passing. In that case, like graves, they serve as points of continuing contact with the dead. The Old Nogales Highway, beginning here in South Tucson, had so many such shrines, so many dead claimed by its twists and turns in the too often drunken night, that many knew it as El Camino del Muerte, the Road of Death.

The murder map of Tucson gives that phrase a new meaning, as does the

San Juan Folklórico at the International Mariachi Conference in Tucson, 1995

shrine built by Peter Valenzuela's Yaqui uncle beside Tenth Avenue just blocks from the Old Nogales Highway. Some people had warned him not to build it there, right in the middle of B-12 Gang territory. His nephew's murderers would surely destroy or deface it, they warned.

They were wrong.

We found the shrine there on the southern edge of urban Tucson, a three-foot-high mound of stone and mortar adorned with a small American flag, a plastic-encased smiling photo of Peter, and a white Yaqui cross bristling with mysterious sticks and fetish bundles. Below it, on the ground, was a plastic basin with dozens of coins.

Like the muralists, Peter's uncle had resisted the numbing repetition and anonymity of barrio murder and had used his art to capture and redirect the power of death. Whether from fear or respect, or both, no one had disturbed Peter Valenzuela's shrine.

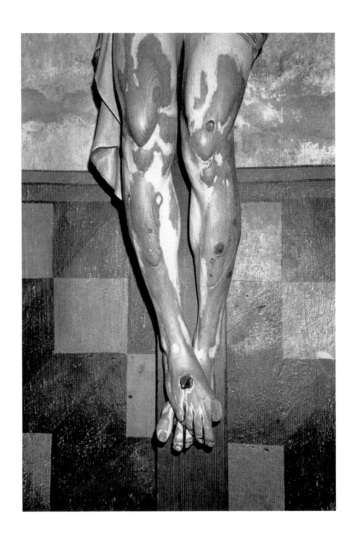

A detail of a Spanish crucifix at the entrance to San Xavier del Bac Mission near Tucson

the mission

The Santa Cruz River runs through the San Xavier District Tohono O'odham Indian Reservation. We did not recognize it, however, suffering as we did from a limited, eastern view that rivers must contain water.

The Santa Cruz does run, in some places and at some times, but not there and not then. Instead, it was a shallow dirt canyon running just to the west and then crossing under the highway, snaking widely through the lower bajada of creosote bushes and mesquite trees. Summer monsoons normally re-create the river, but they had not yet come. One could still trace the currents of the last waters in the sculpted sand bottom. The Santa Cruz is a river that most often flows belowground, sinking ever deeper, trying in vain to hide from an always thirsty Tucson.

My eye did catch a white gleam on the horizon to the west: the white tower and block of the Mission San Xavier del Bac. Framed by a series of scrub-coated hills, the mission presides over the otherwise flat, fine-sand fields of its own district of the Tohono O'odham.

Bac is O'odham for "where the waters gather," but it looked awfully dry, a monotony of creosote, cholla, and mesquite—the constant landscape where the sand is too tight to permit that icon of the Southwest, the saguaro cactus to grow. Most of the homes were charmless boxes of concrete blocks, often accompanied by rusting cars and junk piles.

Cars and buses exit the interstate here, disgorging Mexicans from the south and American and more exotic tourists (French, German, Dutch, Japanese) down from Tucson. We joined them on the road that is now a well maintained extension of the interstate, ending in a vast, sandy parking lot. It was a Sunday, always the busiest day, when the flow of tourists and pilgrims is greatest and is much augmented by locals and visitors who have gathered for one mass or another. The congregation of worshipers inside was matched by the rows of cars and buses outside. The giant mission seemed to have gathered before it an audience of glinting, colorful metal boxes.

Facing the mission on the other side of the parking lot is a substantial brick enclosure containing a series of shops, all run by Native Americans, though few of them are the local Tohono O'odham. A natty Hopi sells the jewelry, baskets, and kachina figures of his own and other Pueblo tribes, and that day a Navajo had set up a jewelry stand near the doors. But the Mexican families crowding around him were far more interested in the album he was showing them, crammed with photos of himself as an all-purpose Indian in dozens of westerns.

"In all those movies, did you ever get to play yourself?" a tiny Mexican mother asked as the Navajo autographed little movie cards for her happy sons.

"No, I never did," he answered half smiling in reflection but without apparent frustration.

Back across the parking lot, nearer the mission, were two sets of flimsy stick and plywood ramadas—snack booths—run by local Indian families. In the partial shadows cast within, dark, round mothers and daughters were slowly but deftly pounding, stretching, and finally tossing ragged circles of fry-bread dough into oil-filled cast-iron pans spitting over mesquite and scrap-wood fires in stoves made from oil drums halved lengthwise. A few quick jerks with a stick and the fry bread is whipped out and set on a paper plate, there to be coated with powdered sugar, honey, cheese, or mounded bits of grilled, chillied meat and melted cheese to make Navajo Tacos. Most visitors bypassed these treats and streamed into the mission itself.

San Xavier's cult arrived here in the Southwest in 1692, more than a century after his death. He was the politically appropriate private devotion of another Jesuit, the Tyrolean Eusebio Francisco Kino, who had hoped to follow San Xavier's path to the Far East. Instead, he came to the northern frontier of New Spain, far from colonial comforts and even the more settled and "cultured" Indians of the center.

This desert was the end of the road for the tireless missionary. He had pressed this far into the northern wilderness, creating a series of missions to bring the Faith, and colonial culture, to the scattered seasonally nomadic bands of Indians. The Spanish called them Papagos (Bean Eaters), a name that stuck until 1985, when the tribe insisted that the outside world call them by their own name for themselves: Tohono O'odham (Desert People).

Though the Jesuits were successful here, however, European power politics brought them to a losing confrontation with the king of Spain, and by the time their Irish captain, Hugo O'Conor, had moved the garrison to what would become Tucson in 1775, the Jesuits had been disappropriated of all their New World holdings. Their Sonoran missions were taken over by the Franciscans. The present San Xavier Mission was built by them toward the end of the eighteenth century, but the name and the saint who lies within are still the Jesuit Francis—Francisco Xavier—himself a missionary to Goa.

One of the original band of Jesuits, Francisco Xavier (like the founder of the order, Ignatius Loyola) was a Basque. Unlike Loyola, however, he was not noted for his learning. On the contrary, he set out for Goa in India in 1542 in the service of the Church and the Portuguese Crown armed with pietistic faith rather than canonical or theological knowledge. According to his biographers, he manifested few ethnographic tendencies during his stint in the Far East. He never learned any local language, and he cared nothing for the wealth of cultural traditions he confronted there.

To judge by all the standard biographies (like *The Saints,* edited by John Coulson), San Francisco did not distinguish among erudite Buddhists, Hindu peasants, and Moslem judges. All were simply pagans to be brought to the right path—a curious common symbol for his multicultural followers.

His own path led him through India to Japan and to an island where he died ten years after his mission began while awaiting permission to enter China. Although—or perhaps because—he died without sacraments or a Christian burial, Francisco was discovered some weeks later, his body incorrupt.

That body is still displayed in the Christian region of Goa in India. Patron of all missionaries, the saint-in-death is reproduced in many countries, but this borderland is home to many of his most devoted followers. Over them stretches a sacred canopy anchored in the north by San Xavier Mission and in the south by another mission in Magdalena de Kino, Sonora. Goa is far away, and the life-sized statues in these twos churches are as close to the saint as one can get. They are sought by thousands of pilgrims and are reproduced in versions anywhere from a few inches to several feet in length. These smaller San Franciscos hold places of honor in the homes and village shrines along and near the road between the two poles.

The devotees of San Francisco Xavier are not uniform. They are Mexican, Mexican American, Tohono O'odham, and to a far lesser extent Anglo. Ethnic and other divisions mark versions of the saint just as surely as the different aspects of Mary and Jesus represented in such varying images as the crowned monarch, the suffering martyr, and the grieving mother each serves as a possible vessel of experience and identity.

San Xavier Mission is one of the most beautiful missions in the New World. It embodies a combination of architectural styles but is most noted for its fabulous painted walls and sculptures. A favorite subject of photographers and regional promoters, it attracts devotees and tourists, and for either sort of traveler the mission might be the destination of a pilgrimage, a voyage that brings together the political and personal aspects of the road.

Certainly the tourist's experience is as structured as the devotee's. Upon entering the mission, one is addressed directly by a loud, disembodied, and patiently instructive recorded voice. It recounts, at regular intervals, the history of the mission and directs attention to the surrounding architectural and artistic details. The colors and forms are dizzying. Polychromatic folk motifs swirl behind the imposing human forms of saints and angels: Mary as the sorrowful mother, a stern San Xavier glowering over the altar, Christ in a typically Spanish passion with lines of blood streaking down from his crown of thorns, and most important, reclining under Christ, San Xavier in death, displayed in an open-front glass casket. All these statues are draped in real clothing. Mary wears a surprisingly joyful, vibrant blue dress, Christ is robed in electric pink, the erect San Xavier is in his black and white bishop's robes, and the recumbent version is draped in glowing purple, black, and white.

Pinned to the saint's robes are *milagros,* tiny metal arms, legs, eyes, hearts. The great majority are requests that the power and empathy of the saint, and the prayers of any who come here, be invoked for the relief from an affliction. Other milagros have been left by grateful people in recognition of miraculous cures performed by virtue of San Xavier's intervention. For whatever reason, many lives are for that moment joined around San Xavier.

The tourists are invited to take photos of the surrounding splendors, and many do. They point their cameras at the colossal projecting wooden angels or the gaily draped Christ or Mary, but most of all of at San Xavier in death.

Maeve took photos as well, but paused on a bench just to the right of San Xavier and next to two young Mexican American women from South Tucson, one of whom had her infant of ten days nestled in her arms. Maeve joined them in happy admiration of the baby girl, who had just been christened with the name Genesis and was cupcaked for the occasion with endless bits of lace frill. In a moment they had all risen and were arranging themselves as photographer and subjects before the saint.

There is nothing sacrilegious about such an act. Had we been in Mexico, in fact, several local photographers would have been making their living by capturing the happy occasion of the child's first visit to the saint. The religious act is taken home, preserved as family memory, and displayed as such among photos of other life crises—some religious, some not.

Photos move in the opposite direction as well, brought from family life into this holy place. Many of the tourists were plainly amazed by the dozens of snapshots among the profusion of objects decorating the saint's robes, not only the milagros of which the voice spoke but also hospital wristbands, pieces of jewelry, and folded bits of paper.

There was nothing overtly religious about the photos. One of them was of a mob of young boys playing and mugging naughtily for the camera. The images were frozen moments of life posed in or before houses, next to a car, on vacation. Some of the tourists were curious enough to turn over the photographs and read the messages often inscribed in English or Spanish on the back. Some inscriptions

A sculpted angel's head on the west wall of San Xavier del Bac Mission

simply identified the people in the picture, but others explained to the saint and to all who came to visit him that those in the pictures were afflicted or faced hazards or dangerous passages of life when luck and protection were especially needed.

As the last clutch of tourists wandered out of the mission into the brilliant sunlight, a young Tohono O'odham couple arrived, bearing a tiny, tightly swathed infant.

"She was just born, I just had her seven hours ago," the mother told Maeve, happily displaying the damp new pilgrim, her hands still gray from birth. This was the child's first stop, beginning its life with a visit to the saint.

The mother touched the body of the saint, lightly caressing the foot, knee, and head. She turned to her husband and, barely touching his face, transferred the blessing to him and then to the baby. She then tucked the hospital bassinet card and wrist bracelet neatly beneath San Xavier's robes. Then they left.

Alongside her offering and those of other mothers—baby photos, impossibly slight hospital wrist bands, even curling sonograms—someone had pinned a clipping from a news magazine with a photograph of two young children: the Smith boys of Union, South Carolina. We recognized them, as any American would have, for their photos had been constantly on TV news reports over the previous weeks, ever since their mother had reported their abduction by a carjacker. After more than a week of frantic searching and the creation of a media-induced sense of national community, the mother confessed that she had in fact murdered her own children, strapping them into their seats and sending the car rolling into a lake.

Over the ensuing months the lake would become a place of pilgrimage, and a shrine would be assembled there to the dead children and to children generally. Photos, of course, but made universal by the addition of many teddy bears, the current symbol not only of children but of parenthood, here gone terribly astray. The Smith children's memorial would become one of a series of ephemeral shrines to an equally ephemeral national community of affliction. The nation mourns, the nation moves on.

But the process had only just begun when some pilgrim had been moved to pluck the title page of the magazine article and transfer the story from a larger and looser America to this ancient corner, perhaps hoping to make sense of it here with the saint. The headline read, "How Could She Do It?"

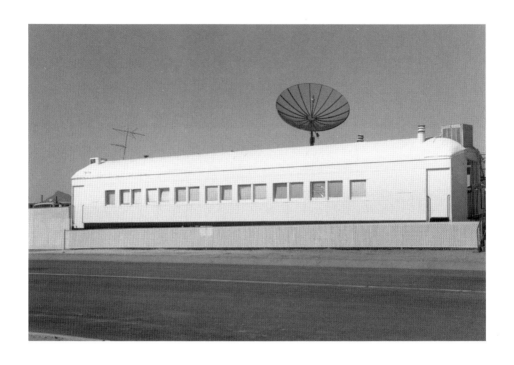

Jimmy's Diner on Business 19 (Nogales Highway) near Tucson

Jimmy's Diner

The menu says it is an early 1900s railroad car. Actually there are two cars, both brilliant white, parked one behind the other on the Old Nogales Highway just south of the Desert Diamond Casino on the eastern edge of the San Xavier Reservation. The front car is the diner; the one behind is Jimmy Veck's living quarters. A third, unpainted car has just found its way into the yard, recently enclosed by the Indians with a gleaming white chain-link fence, apparently to separate Jimmy's junk from their own.

"I built it myself," Jimmy told me.

He meant the interior of the dining car, but Jimmy has assembled a whole world here. Visitors mount a ramp to enter the front end and find themselves in a narrow passage that takes them by the ersatz-archaic cash register, under the TV perched on a sagging metal shelf above—mercifully, never turned on—and into the dining room, with its high-backed, vinyl-seated dining chairs clustered around ten tables bolted to the wall as if the car were still in motion. Above, the barrel-vaulted ceiling is sectioned by metal strips framing flowered and buttoned fabric in browns and blues. That day the late lunch crowd was busily laying into barbecued beef.

Everybody looked local; nobody was. They were an assortment of men with baseball caps whom the road had brought from different places and for different reasons.

Roger, a small, quiet man of about fifty, came to Arizona twenty years ago from upstate New York looking for his idea of the West. Now he lives just a bit down the road in Sahuarita and plays music with a band called the Country Outlaw. He was looking forward to their next big gig: New Year's Eve at the Green Valley Trailer Court.

"Roger has been coming in for a long time," said Jane, the pretty young waitress. "But in the beginning he had nothing to say, never opened his mouth. So one day I told him that if he didn't stop raising a ruckus I was goin' to throw him out of here! Well, that sort of opened him up and, by God, he's got a personality now!" So does everyone here, it seems.

Jane was herself another accidental pilgrim.

"I came here for lunch one time, and I left a check to pay for it with my phone number on it. A few days later my phone rings at six thirty in the morning. It was Jimmy. He said, 'If you want to work here, you have to be here by seven o'clock.'"

She had not asked for a job, but she showed up anyway and had been here for a year, badgering the reticent and otherwise aiding her boss in his primary mission: creating an ephemeral community on the edge of the desert, like the plants that shoot up here after a rainstorm.

Jimmy himself rose from his early afternoon nap and lumbered through his stage set, his tall, heavy frame swelling beneath the apron, and his pin-striped railroad engineer's cap framing a broad, pink-cheeked, gray-bearded, satisfied face. Sinking comfortably into one of his upholstered seats, he recounted in spare phrases how he came to be here. Born in Texas, he had been sent as a young man to his uncle's farm near Tucson but early had a desire to go into the restaurant business.

"I like people," he explained.

A railroad enthusiast and road romantic, he found the answer to his dreams abandoned in the desert just south of Tucson: railroad cars left there to the slow decay of the Southwest. With the aid of a friend who was a welder and mechanic, Jimmy gave the cars, and himself, a new life. Unconstrained by tracks, he hitched his diner to a truck and hauled it to California. That dream soured, so a few years later he returned to Tucson. He had parked for some time on Benson Highway, near the airport, but seems to have found his proper niche here, at least for a while. His business card, which promises a "New Concept in Dining," is decorated with an alluring violet line drawing of his dining car floating above—not on—railroad tracks and still attached to a truck cab, as if threatening to move off any moment from the address printed below.

No doubt thinking about that very issue, Jimmy told the story of a small restaurant owner in Tucson who had built up a big clientele and had then moved down the street to larger quarters.

"But it didn't work out, and after a while he moved back."

Joe, a young man dressed hopefully in a business suit, was skeptical. "Maybe there were other reasons," he said.

One of Jimmy's regulars, Joe had been learning about business and life from his wife, who had just gotten a job with Mary Kay Cosmetics.

"You see, they're not cosmetics, they are skin care products," he earnestly informed us.

He had bought more than that line. While Jimmy saw life and fortune as a restless search for the perfect place and moment, Joe was more inclined to believe in a world, an America, of infinite growth, of being not just your own boss but the boss of others in an endlessly growing pyramid. To succeed, one always moved forward and up, not just down the road, like Jimmy.

But Jimmy is an artist as well as a businessman. Having built his own stage, he cajoles others to perform on it. In that work he has a more than able assistant in Jane. Though he had somehow known that she was destined to work for him, nothing about Jane (a retro hippie with a dozen rings in each ear) suggested that she would fit into this world.

"I love working here," she told us. "I live near the university, and coming here every morning is like going to another planet. This is the last grazing ground of the American dinosaur."

This line was delivered for the crowd as she flipped another platter of barbecue beef before a happy trucker. Everyone smiled in self-recognition.

"I used to work for a vegetarian restaurant," she continued. "I really appreciate the contrast. Nobody in here is a vegetarian. Nobody worries about cholesterol. Does anyone here think about cholesterol?"

She spun around to face her audience. To a man, each one laughed beneath his cap brim and bent happily to his lunch. One of their number, John, drawled in Texas Panhandle the expected response: "They keep changin' their minds anyway. Probably cholesterol will turn out to be good for you."

John answered my question about what had brought him here with a fuller response than even I had hoped for.

"I don't know if you want to get into that, because it was the Lord who brought me here."

He was hesitant to take that rhetorical path until he knew he had found a listener. I settled down across from him with my lemonade, and he began, his evangelically clean-shaven face still smiling beneath a red cap emblazoned with the name of his new home: Arizona. American pilgrims do not always need a church.

"God came to me on January first, 1992. I was working in Houston, Texas, and the Lord told me to leave there. He purposed me to come this way. All I can tell you is that he is going to do something big in the southwestern desert, maybe a coming together of true Christians, like a revival, before the coming end of the world."

He was dreamy and still smiling as he described his own vision of Armageddon. I was not sure whether this oracle knew more than he was saying of the Lord's plans.

"You see, He had spoken to me years before, when I was twelve. I was sitting on the ground and the Lord spoke to me. He told me that He was going to destroy cities in New York, Florida, and California. They would be destroyed in a great conflagration. When He was telling me this, He caused my fingers to move in the dirt. That was the destruction of the cities.

"But I had forgotten all that. Thirty years later, last year, He released me to remember. I was sitting on a beach and I had my hand in the sand, and when I moved my fingers through the sand I remembered what He had told me about the fires, about the destruction. He released me to remember."

John's tale struck me as a curious religious version of the suppressed memory syndrome, a condition usually associated with childhood sexual abuse. The resemblance is more than superficial. John's memory of contact with God was physical, marked by a sensuality of fingers wiggling in sand that in fact rekindled the memory. But John's memory would, in his case, send him back to the powerful Father.

"The Lord took control of my life," he continued. "He told me to leave my job, leave everything [including a fourth wife] and head this way, toward the desert. I grew a big beard and I never washed and I just wandered all through the Southwest. Went to California, went to Mexico. When I was down there I got terribly drunk, and my truck broke down. I didn't know what to do, and I had no way out of there. The Lord came to my aid. Somehow—I can't tell you how—I got a motorcycle, that Harley parked out there. I had no money, so I cannot tell you how I got it, but somehow I did. I am happy now in obedience to the Lord. He released me to shave off my beard and to clean myself up, and I came straight up to this place because this is where the Lord wants me to work."

He did not mean his paying job, which, he told me, was wiring delivery systems for Hughes Missile Systems just across the road.

"I find people who want to hear my message and I help them, like an Indian I met here. I lived with him in an apartment in Tucson for a couple of months. He was weak. He needed to sever from his family. They were keeping him down. I tried to help him, got him off drink for a while, but in the end he went back to them and the drink."

I supposed John was between cases. He was living in motels and, not unlike us, was traveling up and down the highway falling into conversations with lost strangers.

"I only tell my message to people who are ready to hear it. Most people are good, but they are lost and ignorant of the Lord's purpose. The enemy," he said, still smiling, "are the New Agers and the satanists with the 666."

While I contemplated this formulation, John rose and, radiating good will, said good-bye and headed back to his missile systems.

Jane came over and refilled my lemonade.

"Say," she said, "you were lost in the Jesus zone."

I liked the phrase and the notion of a parallel geography it implied: American cultural regions, in this case like the Bible Belt, replaced by stacked dimensions defined by language: the business zone, the golf zone, the football zone, the Jesus zone. It does not matter where you are, and often you cannot tell just by knowing whom your talking to, but if you press the right verbal button, you find yourself rocketed into a very specific universe, a monoculture.

Months later we returned to Jimmy's. It was humming with a steady stream of regulars and passers-by on an already blazing hot summer Sunday morning. Jane was there and in fine form, wearing a skintight flowered skirt and a black tank top, and only seven sets of earrings framed by her pigtails. Her big hazel eyes were deceptively dreamy as she passed from table to table, serving and joking, even plopping down into a chair across from one regular or another to chat for a moment. However often she paused or quipped, she managed to serve everyone deftly and easily, wise-cracking all the while with seasoned veteran or newcomer regardless of class, color, or creed.

I had already missed the morning's religious incident. It did not involve the Jesus zone this time. John, the wandering evangelist, had apparently wired his last missile delivery system some months before, mounted his Harley, and headed wherever the Lord "purposed" him.

That morning it was John's nemesis who had appeared on this desert stage.

"Do you know that family of satanists?"

Jane had poured a couple's coffee and had then sunk down into the chair opposite while they decided whether or not to go, as usual, for the hobo's special: an egg and sausage burrito with home fries, refried beans, and homemade salsa for $1.70.

"They all have 666 tattooed on their foreheads. That's right," she continued, "they always come in the morning and stay for hours just drinking coffee."

Jimmy had wandered over and sat down at my table to see how the author was getting along, as well as to chat with the couple across the way, old friends as it turned out. He added more detail on the satanists.

"Yeah, they come in early every morning and drink a lot of coffee."

He was most struck, however, by the parental control over even the toddler.

"They just put that baby on the table and he doesn't move. 'How do you get him to do that?' I asked them. So the old man says, 'We started him off on the fridge.'"

"Well," Jane continued, "they were here as usual—over there—this morning. I was giving the man a refill, and I guess I just slammed it down in front of him. So he looks up at me and says, 'You don't like us because of our religion.'

"So I said to him, 'If pigs flew out of Jimmy Veck's butt and you decided to worship them, it wouldn't matter a damn to me. I don't like you because you never tip.'"

Giant saguaro near Continental, Arizona

the edge of the res

The Desert Diamond Casino—a vast white plastic bubble surrounded by jammed parking lots—sits on the Nogales Highway on the edge of the San Xavier Reservation a few miles east of the mission and just a few hundred yards from Jimmy's Diner. My first visit was late on a Sunday morning. It was as bustling as the mission and the diner but with a bigger crowd and, no doubt, a higher percentage of believers.

The passage from blinding white stillness outside into the cool, dark, cacophonous whirl of the great gambling hall was more than a little disorienting. I nearly walked into the rear end of a teal green Pontiac Firebird perched there on a dais, the grand prize in some game of fortune.

After my eyes and ears had adjusted, I surveyed the huge room stretching out before me. It was equipped with a snack bar, an automatic teller, and a change machine, but most of it was taken up by banks of coin-operated gambling machines—slots, stud poker, and the like—demanding anywhere from twenty-five cents to a dollar a throw. Every machine responded to the human touch with lights, bells, whistles, and the occasional whoosh of coins or tokens, none of which seemed to threaten the concentration of the several hundred souls cranking their arms or pressing their buttons. The ratio of women to men was about two to one, all, by appearance, from the working and the lower middle classes.

In the back of the hall was another, smaller room, nearly serene and intimate by contrast. There were no machine noises. Instead, the Beach Boys' "Wouldn't It Be Nice" wafted softly over dealerless tables of electronic blackjack. Here there were more men than women, but they were equally intent on the project before them. It was mainly men again in another large room, but here they were playing with real cards and real dealers. Finally, around another corner, I found the bingo hall, where nearly three hundred people sat watching and listening for their numbers.

Throughout this prefab big top, men and women fed their machines or tables with sober determination, barely smiling when they won small and often speeding up when they lost. They spoke little and smoked a lot. It was hard to tell if they were having a good time, but they sure were busy.

Casinos have spread farther and faster across Native America than did the fabled Ghost Dance. From coast to coast, non-Indian Americans now flock onto reservations not to absorb Indian culture but to gamble. In its first two years the Desert Diamond Casino took in nearly $20 million, and the profits have been sitting in banks awaiting a master plan that will make the best use of such funds in a world whose main income had previously been federal subsidies of one kind or another.

The money goes to the Tohono O'odham Nation, consisting of about 13,000 people. But that entity, which is governed by a tribal council, is divided into two increasingly fractious units. The main reservation is a huge tract of desert with widely scattered villages that begins about thirty miles west of Tucson and borders on Mexico for many miles. Then there is the more compact Xavier District, a tourist attraction because of the mission and now the casino. The proximity to

Tucson and the roads south—from the first Spanish trail to I-19—have made the San Xavier district a different world from that of the main reservation.

Edward Encinas, director of the San Xavier District's Elderly Program, looks forward to a time when those differences are resolved by divorce and the people of the San Xavier District are recognized as a distinct tribe. I met him in the just-completed Center for the Elderly, the first tangible benefit from the millions taken in at the casino. The handsome structure stood in stark contrast to the prefab district offices and cinder-block school next door. They were emblems of poverty and government dependence; the new center spoke of hope for the future.

Edward, a slim, soft-spoken man of forty-seven, was justly proud.

"It was built of stones taken down from nearby Black Mountain—our sacred peak—by professional work crews, but the last several were brought down by members of the reservation by hand so that the building could feel more their own."

We talked about his work with the elderly but also about the more general past and future of his place and people.

"Things have changed in my life here. The elders often talk about the water level, and I myself remember wells being fifty feet deep. Now the water is two to three hundred feet down, and our pumps can't even reach it. Most of our farming stopped because of that. The land is so dry now, but I remember how green it was every summer. Just down there by the river were wooded areas. The water ran freely, and there was a lot of Bermuda grass. That was about forty years ago. There was much more water in the river then. Our people used to grow their own crops when I was growing up, people from that area [his eyes turned southwest, toward the big reservation] would come down here in the summer and then go back. School would end and we'd move into the fields to grow peas, chiles, and sugarcane. You know, that's all we lived on in those days. We never ran to the store. We just stayed here. It was a time for relatives and friends to get together. We worked together in harvest teams, roasting corn and doing whatever needed to be done. In our section there were about seven families living near one another in the summer, but they came from different winter directions.

"I really miss those days. It was all green around here. When the summer ended, we'd move back to our regular winter houses. All that stopped finally about twenty years ago. Now the freeway's there and nothing but dry, dry weeds."

Water has always been an issue here. In the early days of the reservation, the problem was Anglo ranchers settling around the perimeter of the Indians' land and drawing off their water. More recently it has been the far greater use of water by the pecan growers and the nearby copper mines, whose promise of mineral wealth has drawn thousands to the region. The rubble of their giant pits now rises like flat-topped, terraced mountains, forming a peculiar range that dominates the western vista for some miles beginning just south of the reservation. Several of the mines are, in fact, tenants of the O'odham.

"Some of our people see them as a source of revenue. There used to be a lot of them worked in the mines, but now there are only about five or six from the village here. They use all the water, and they are dumping waste that will be there forever. It's not worth what it's doing to the land."

He was inclined to see relations with the U.S. government in a similar light.

"The same thing happened with the road. The Department of Transportation thought it would be so easy. They tried to pay the Indian landowners cheap compared to the city, to take advantage."

But the increasingly sophisticated San Xavier district leadership held up the completion of the highway for some time, until their price had been reached.

"And that highway has brought change," Encinas continued. "Now there's access to the Papago Road, and that causes problems with non-Indians coming in and dumping, or cutting wood. And the Department of Transportation doesn't check the fences often enough. Non-Indians cut them for various illegal activities and our cattle get on the road and there are accidents, and the stock owners could get sued for damage to vehicles and passengers."

But the same highway brought the promise of increased tourism, and Edward hoped his district could take further advantage of it.

"The government may get rid of gaming in seven or eight years, and we can't be dependent on it. We need to start looking at other sorts of revenues, invest in something. For about one million we can turn the area in front of the church into a park with running water and more parking for tourists."

In this, as in all things, it seemed to Edward that the Tohono O'odham Nation was the big stumbling block. Water was still—will always be—the crucial issue. The San Xavier District does not have its own rights to the new water being brought into the region from the Colorado River (the Central Arizona Project water) but instead depends on what it perceives to be an unsympathetic tribal government miles away in Sells.

"Our farms need help, and they say no. There have always been differences between the main reservation and us, and now, with arguments about water rights and the casino, it's worse. They're always saying, 'You guys are from near Tucson.' They don't like to give us anything—our fair share—because they figure we have more opportunity, being near Tucson. The casino was built here because it's close to the airport. The Nation manages the casino, but it is on our district land."

In the meantime, Edward is busy with the elderly. They have weekly meetings and activities, and Edward takes groups of his clients on van trips. Sometimes they go as far as New Mexico, but more often the excursions are local.

"Last week," he told me, "we went to the southwest portion of the district. There used to be a village there. Some of my clients grew up there and hadn't seen it in fifty years. When they went out there, they were shocked to see the forest gone, cut by outsiders. It was sad to see."

They also go to Magdalena de Kino in Sonora, the southern end of San Francisco Xavier's sacred territory. Edward, however, gave the local saint prominence.

"The saint there is named after the one here, and people from down there come here too.

"We also go down to Nogales, Sonora, for shopping trips but especially to prepare for the Day of the Dead. We go to a store in Nogales, Sonora—a little flower shop—and to another for crepe paper for wreaths."

He got one from a closet to show me.

"November 2, All Souls Day, comes from Spanish culture, and for the whole month of October the old people here are busy making wreaths for their relatives. You see, we share a lot of culture with the Mexicans. The food, music, and prayers in Mexico are like ours."

In fact, there are a few hundred O'odham living in Mexico in isolated parts of Sonora, where, by all accounts, they have fared even worse than here. They suffer discrimination there, too, but with no offsetting special rights. They tell stories of *federales* arriving to take their cattle.

The O'odham in Arizona have their own problems. Beyond the usual poverty there is a high rate of morbid obesity and an correspondingly high incidence of diabetes. There are also the same problems found in the nearby urban world, for which Edward's solution was as cultural as those of muralist Antonio Pazos and Fernando Sanchez, the mariachi.

"Drugs are affecting us a lot. I have some boys that I work with that I hope will be our spiritual leaders. They are starting to get involved in our ceremonies. One is about seventeen, and another is about twenty. They are learning the traditional songs and are often involved in ceremonies. It is very important to keep our traditions. I stress that in our gatherings, to offer prayers, reburial ceremonies, anniversaries, at death. I tell the elders that we need to talk about our traditions and culture, to encourage the youth to continue their studies.

"We pray for those kids who are into the other things. I hope they're just trying it out and something will help them, that they'll find out it's not good for them. They are getting hurt, getting killed.

"They have gang colors. In Native American culture, colors have a meaning to us. We use them in our ceremonies. It's not our way of life to think a blue color can get you hurt.

"What's happening now is not our way of life. There was a boy buried here three years ago who was shot in town by one of our boys. People were coming out and desecrating that boy's grave. They put a red scarf on the grave cross. It is not right; they should let him rest in peace. The gangs come here to recruit. There's been one drive-by. They flashed their weapons and shot into the air."

I asked Edward where he hoped things might be in twenty years' time.

"I hope that the new generation is learning from what's happening. We tried to educate them so that they'll be strong to continue to protect our land. And if we're not successful now in getting back what's rightfully ours, I hope they continue the fight.

"I hope that we no longer have the mines, and that most of all we succeed in our secession. Next time we will go to Congress and argue for historical separation. Originally we were a separate entity. When the agency—the Bureau of Indian Affairs—was first here, we were already by ourselves."

"And the casino?" I asked.

"According to the compact, the district gets a little more if we split. That's why they don't want to let us go. They're afraid we will get our own compact with the state and own the casino."

I asked him if he went to the casino himself.

"No," he laughed. "I go to gamble at Pasqua Yaqui," referring to the other Indian tribe and casino in the region.

"I took the elderly group there once, and I gamble there myself. You know, not to be seen here. But there were ten or fifteen O'odham there!"

I said good-bye to Edward and walked over to the mission, a few hundred yards away, for a quick check on the ever-changing assemblage of photos and messages left in the mortuary chapel and on the blanket covering the effigy of the saint. I then drove across the reservation for another view of that other place of favors: the casino. Perhaps it was because I went from one to the other that I was struck by the strange symmetry of these two great white edifices rising from the desert.

The mission was built by the Spanish alongside their imperial road, linking the O'odham there to the outside world and defining their boundaries with respect to their fellow Indians. It still sits in the center of their world. Served now by Franciscans, it attracts thousands of tourists, though they leave little money for the O'odham.

Now, along the newer road, another great mediator has risen: the casino. But that sits at the edge, not the center, of the local world, sapping millions from tourists and even more from the surrounding lower and middle classes. That aquifer never seems to dry up.

Inside, the scene was as before, though the clientele does change subtly according to a weekly cycle.

"The Mexicans come on Friday and Saturday nights," a young floor manager told me, himself a Chicano from near Yuma.

"It's a good job," he went on to say. "Nothing much happens here, except sometimes two customers might fight over a machine. Like, one of them thinks it's hers!"

The woman nearest us, a bony fifty-year-old blonde, was feeding her poker machine with speed and dexterity, a cloud of cigarette smoke extending her beehive hairdo. She reached the end of her pile and, without turning away from her machine, whipped a twenty-dollar bill behind her for the passing attendant. The heavy, dark O'odham girl silently took the money, put a paper cup full of quarters into the player's hand, and wheeled her cart toward the next customer.

An abandoned structure off Old Nogales Highway near Summit, Arizona

Delia

The Old Nogales Highway is a road that, like the fabled Route 66, shares in an American romance different from that of the interstate. Here, the up-to-date sits awkwardly, unstylishly cheek by jowl with the embarrassingly eccentric and the downright ugly, like a strange shore littered with the flotsam and jetsam of dying personal dreams and renowned half-wonders: "Only one hundred and fifty miles to the 'Thing!'"

The road begins with the poverty and exuberance of South Tucson, but the more open road south, though sparser, is equally colorful. After we passed the Desert Diamond Casino and Jimmy's Diner, there was the A Auto salvage yard, over which floats the impaled carcass of a Ford or Chevy; a garage whose stack of retreads adds a third dimension to the "ruckus" checkerboard low-rider mural behind it; and so on.

Naturally, we were drawn to this road. As an artist, Maeve's eye for the telling fragment leads her to the small object, like the hair braid discovered in the sand outside a Mexican church, to which she later joined gilded chili peppers and bits of Irish bog to form a sort of reliquary collage. But she is also drawn to the larger fragments, like the splintered world along this road. As for me, like a bandit I, too, tend to avoid the center.

The people along this road are, of course, far from remote, though they may be increasingly distant from a certain idea of America. And the roads they live along, like the Nogales Highway and even more so the Old Nogales Highway, no longer go anywhere. They lie now in pieces, shattered by the interstate just like downtown Tucson's barrios, where all that remains of the Old Pueblo are remnant barrios separated from one another by parking lots, gleaming office towers, and streets that have become highways feeding into that same voracious interstate.

So there is no choice for the traveler now, no way to avoid that road and maintain an illusion of possibility, of getting to Mexico by some other means. At best one compromises, zigzagging back and forth between surviving segments of Old Nogales Highway or the Nogales Highway until an impasse is reached and then retracing one's path to I-19.

It might have been an archaeological site. Traveling south along the Nogales Highway (a.k.a. "Business 19"), just a few miles south of the reservation, we passed the last few commercial enterprises, which now tempt only local traffic: the Mexico Way Market, the Top Hat Saloon, and the ruins of Guacho's Tires.

On the western side of the road, only partially hidden behind a thin curtain of mesquite, was another sort of remnant: a small, abandoned stone house. Scattered around the half-acre chain-link-fenced yard were structures of uncertain form, material, and purpose. A defunct miniature golf course, perhaps? Not so, as we discovered on closer inspection.

The small house was clearly home-made. Folklorists call it vernacular architecture. The walls were of random stones and cement, and one of them was cracking and preparing to part company from the others. The castellated roof was echoed in a series of realized and abandoned projects: a twenty-foot-long segment of high wall, a tiny castle, a well, a low running wall with small, colorful stones arranged to read "1967 Delia."

The house was also named, again in small stones, God's Little Acre. But the name Delia—written in pebbles—reappeared on unexpected corners throughout the site. (Somebody's Rosebud?)

All the works beyond the house were made of green bottles laid on their sides and held together with cement. The most startling were the two full-sized wigwams.

"She started with them wigwams," a neighbor told me. "One day she was out there with a barrow full of green bottles. 'I know what I'm gonna do with these bottles now,' she told me, and she went and built them wigwams."

I had knocked on the door of his small prefab house ringed with toys and a bedspread hammock. A beautiful young Mexican woman eyed me suspiciously from the gloom within.

"I'll get my father-in-law," she said.

She did, and out he came, a bent, good-natured fellow with two or three days of white stubble, peeling skin, and a heavy hand that occasionally dropped in almost Italian emphasis. Did he know the occupant and builder of the follies across the way?

He did indeed. There *was* a Delia, and it was she herself who built it all, though with the help of a series of men who "came on the rails there," he said, pointing to the railroad tracks that run parallel to the highway from the Mexican border to Tucson.

The house was of wood, standard issue, but she had surrounded it with walls of her own in fabulous stone. Then the house had grown an exterior courtyard wall, and as the neighbor explained, it had spread out from there.

The surviving array was impressively, suggestively random. An unremarkable little roofed well had been made strange by the addition of a full-sized cement torso of a woman—a mermaid, or Delia herself?—sunk in the high grass nearby. A bright blue bra had been painted over nippleless breasts. The wigwams presided over the back of the yard, standing a few feet apart and perfectly complete. The exposed bottoms of hundreds of green bottles glinted painfully in the July sun.

"Were they intended for any particular use?" I asked.

He looked at me with the disdain the question deserved. "Didn't you ever see someone paint a picture of the landscape just because he wanted to? Well that's what Delia did. She just wanted to build them wigwams."

"When did she do all that?"

Another rebuff.

"Dates? You want dates? Well, I'm no good for that. And besides, I'm having enough problems with my own dates. I'm trying to write up my background."

Fair enough, I thought. "What is your background?"

Despite the gestures, he was not Italian but a true Anglo and, like so many here, from the Midwest.

"I came here in 1951 from Illinois. I sold the farm for a dollar—all I wanted was the car—and I came down here to start over. I went in with a couple of guys who were into mines—silver, zinc, copper.

"They sent me out to look for silver, and I told them, 'Hey, what do I know about this stuff? I'm an easterner.' Meanwhile, those two were havin' a sleepin' contest.

"Well, I had already sold a farm for a dollar, so I wasn't gonna get bitten again. I got right outa that business."

He jerked a massive thumb over his shoulder to make the point, beaming brightly into the afternoon glare.

His story was told, but Delia remained elusive. She had died, but he couldn't say when. The house, land, and attachments had been left to a relative in San Diego, and a realtor had bought the property.

"She wants to buy up all this land," he spat, sweeping his hand over a series of baked, weed-choked sandlots that flanked the small dead-end street. Beyond, uninterrupted desert stretched to mountains mutilated by the copper mines.

"Did you know her well—Delia?" I asked.

His face brightened like a happy gargoyle. "Well, she did tell a woman who was there with her that she intended to marry me."

Perhaps Delia is better left like that, obliquely remembered by an old man and named in stones on the fragmentary ruins of a very small empire. An "outsider artist" as the galleries call them now, whose impulses were satisfied with a series of men "off the rails" and projects in bottles and stones. No doubt these traces of God's Little Acre will be effaced by the acquisitive realtor or the next dreamer or pilgrim to buy this lot on the Nogales Highway.

As for the neighbor, Delia comes and goes from his musings, like his Illinois farm, as he sits in the television-lit gloom of his prefab, looking into his own background. I bid him good-bye and good luck.

"Thanks," he answered, "but I need more than good luck. I need good looks, and it's too late for that."

A roper's mailbox in Sahuarita, Arizona

the three Mikes

I first met Mike Murat at a roping at the Wanabe Arena in Sahuarita, just behind the Tortilla Factory and Cafe. He was sitting in a wheelchair a few yards away, like someone new to that accommodation, his huge body wedged in unaccustomed confinement and one wrapped, medically shod foot propped awkwardly out in front. He had been watching the last pair of ropers particularly closely, and, leaning out of his chair toward the fence, he yelled some post-play advice to a frustrated young boy walking his palomino slowly along the other side of the fence.

"You're not waiting long enough."

The boy paid no attention and, yanking petulantly on the reins, trotted out of easy earshot. Mike nearly bounced out of the chair with exasperated laughter.

"That little one," he said to anyone who would listen, "he's a real wizard, like I haven't done this!"

I shook my head with a fellow parent's compassion and asked him if he had done much roping himself. He laughed again and, turning his round red face in my direction, beamed happily through his mustache. He raised his right fist, cocking a massive thumb. The top half was missing, a badge of membership in the fraternity. The roper's salute.

The Wanabe is among the more informal arenas in the area, a rough dirt oval in what might be called the Felix family compound: a couple of brick homes, trailers, and of course the Tortilla Factory and Cafe, all amid a few cattle-worried acres just three miles south of Sahuarita on the Old Nogales Highway. If you come to the tortilla factory in the morning, you can watch two women, as big and comfortable-looking as old sofas, hand-stretching and grilling tortillas by the dozen. You'd also be well advised to stay and try a *carne seca* burro—spicy, sun-dried meat wrapped in a large flour tortilla.

By late morning the dirt lot outside the arena was crammed with pickups and horse trailers, and dozens of families had found their places in lawn chairs around the fence. Their attention to the events, which continue at a nearly dreamy pace throughout the day, was often desultory. There were, after all, dozens of entrants, and any particular family in the audience may have been simply waiting—like Mike—for their own son, husband, father, or occasionally daughter to compete.

In the meantime, they amused themselves by gabbing, strolling, or lunching on burros and tamales sold by the proprietors from a small stand. Whole picnicking families lounged under mesquites, and the next generation of ropers and cowboys was in formation: a boy of five earnestly lassoing his grandfather's boot, three young teenaged girls competing in an intermission barrel race, and most entertainingly, a group of seven small children—one longhaired girl among them—taking turns riding a "bull."

Their mount was an old oil drum suspended by three ropes from trees next to the arena. Each child would climb on in turn, find his seat on the ragged sheepskin-rug saddle, slip one hand under the rope rein, and raise the other for balance, like any good bronc or bull rider. Then other children would yank on the ropes with all their might, sending the oil drum into convulsive hops and swings.

The intensity with which these kids pursued their apprenticeship gives credence to one roper parent's words: "I built an arena at home, and I'm going to build

A contestant waits his turn at a roping, Rio Rico, Arizona

a bull-riding arena too. It's for the kids, really. It gives them something to occupy them, something they can be interested in. It keeps them out of gangs, anyway. Yeah, my brother sent his son out here to get him away from the barrio and the gangs in Tucson. We're only twelve miles away, but it's a whole different world."

As a spectator sport, roping is easy enough for the novice to follow. A gate swings open and a young steer bolts out and tears across the arena, pursued by two riders swinging lassos in the air. One of them, the header, drops his rope over the steer's horns and pulls his horse up short, slowing and turning the steer so that the second man, the heeler, can accomplish the trickier task of throwing his loop under the moving hind legs of his quarry and, pulling up sharply, catch one or both limbs in a noose. Then, if all goes well, the steer flops over on his side and the event is over. The announcer calls out the number of seconds the team took to complete their task, and then the next steer is released, with another team in pursuit trying to do exactly the same thing, only faster. And so on through the afternoon.

But, of course, either roper—most often the heeler—can miss his running target, or the steer can shake off a noose before it's tightened and thus elude capture.

That's what happened with the boy, who turned out to be Mike's grandson, Michael Anthony, only eleven years old and already an avid roper. His lasso had found the horns all right, but he had trouble holding and directing the steer. Before his partner could get his loop under its heels, the animal had thrown off Michael Anthony's rope and headed for the far end of the arena. Hence Big Mike's critique.

"That young one is coming along," Mike explained of his grandson, "but he needs more patience. And you can't tell him anything! Dear God, he knows it all already and he's only eleven!" Mike laughed despite himself, obviously enjoying the kid's muleheadedness.

"The other one there," he said, pointing to a handsome teenager in a bold black and white cowboy shirt, ready at the gate, "he's my youngest son, Michael Angel, and he's really gettin' good."

The gate flew open and Michael Angel charged out behind an older, heavyset man who dropped the lasso over the frightened steer's horns and ground to a near halt as his young partner deftly slipped his rope under the animal's hind legs and pulled it taut. Suspended in the air for a split second, the steer swung sideways and then thudded in the dust.

Meanwhile, big Mike, the proud father, had noticed my videocamera.

"Did you get them on film there?" he asked.

I told him that I had filmed all the riders since my arrival and promised to deliver a copy to his home.

"I was definitely born into this," Mike said as we turned back to the action, "on a ranch out near Benson. That's real cattle country. My mom's people—it would have been her grandparents—had come up from Mexico to Tubac in the late 1800s. They had a small ranch there somewhere, but it was rough, man. The Apaches were always attackin', and an uncle of my mom's was killed by the Indians right there by the Elefante. They burned the grass around him and shot him full of arrows.

"My grandfather decided to leave there, and they came out to Benson in a wagon with eleven kids. They stopped for water at a well in the Rincons, near Colossal Cave, and when they had gone on about two miles they realized that one of my uncles was missing. I guess he had fallen off the wagon when they bumped over some rock. So a couple of them rode back, and there he was, all wrapped in his diapers and blankets by the side of the road. Lucky the coyotes didn't get him.

"That was a hard life there, too, but I guess it was a good one. My mother remembers Pancho Villa coming through in 1915 or 1916, when she was a little girl."

Mike's father's story was different.

"He was from Nogales, Sonora, but his people had come up from further south. My great-great-grandfather had come to Mexico with Maximilian. That's how come we have a French name, Murat.

"Anyway, Dad came from Nogales. His mom and dad passed away, and when he was thirteen he walked across [the border]. The railroad gave him a job as a water boy. He wore a yoke with two buckets, with a dipper in each one. He would walk along the line, and as he'd go along, the workers would take drinks from his buckets. He stayed with the railroad for the rest of his life, and when he passed away, fifty-two years later, he was a bridge-building foreman here in Tucson."

Though he admired his father's diligence, the unpredictable life of the cowboy very early captured Mike's imagination, and he left his home in Tucson in 1949 at the age of thirteen to live with an uncle on the homestead. He lived on the ranch there "like a wild Indian," but he earned his keep.

"Roping was work. You would rope steers, like they do in the arena there, on the range so you could dose them with medicine. And the guys that competed in ropings were the same cowboys that did it on the ranch. Now, most of these guys you see here never worked near cows. They're drugstore cowboys, you'd say. And a lot of them think it's the gear that will make them good. They'll spend a thousand dollars on a saddle. I remember when I was a kid on the homestead I was always looking in the catalogues at the real fancy boots. Boy, I wanted them. But one time I showed the picture to my uncle, and he said, 'Boy, you can spend your money on the fanciest pair of boots you can find, but that won't make you a better roper. I'll out-cowboy you barefoot every time!' And he was right, man. It's practice that makes you a roper, not boots, saddles, or fancy trailers."

Apparently Mike had had plenty of practice.

"I left school at fifteen. I didn't go all that often and when I did, I didn't learn much anyway. I joined up with an uncle and we cowboyed for Boquillas Land and Cattle Company in the San Pedro valley and in New Mexico for the Victoria Cattle Company. I remember driving the cattle through the snow. I was only a kid, but I worked like a man and got the same wages—twenty-five dollars a month and all the beans you could eat.

"Yeah, beans. But them old cowboys, if they were running short of beef, they'd just run a cow till it broke a leg, then we'd have to butcher him, and we'd be eating meat alright! They rolled up the meat in a tarp and stuck it under the bed in the summertime. It would keep a long time that way. Or they'd jerky it up. We had cheese, too, but it wasn't easy to get the milk with the cows out there. You'd have to hold on to one teat in the air while she jumped around, and you'd get a little milk at a time."

The roping at the Wanabe Arena was winding up. The five-year-old winner of the cash raffle was announced, and the victors of the roping competitions claimed their cash prizes, halters, and saddles while posing for family photos. It was a real neighborly affair, and to judge by appearances we were the only strangers in the crowd. The three Mikes packed up their horses, mounted their pickup, and headed north and west into the desert, urging us again to visit.

"I've got my own little arena. We're out in the country. It's real beautiful."

Some days later we made our way, videotape in hand, out to their digs about eight miles southwest of Tucson, not far from the new Yaqui reservation.

Mike, grinning as usual, swung himself up to our car on a pair of crutches. We were standing stunned before the world he had assembled for himself and his namesakes.

"I came back to Tucson two years ago. See, I had been in California, near L.A., for almost thirty years. My co'padre had retired here. That's his brick house you passed on the way in. He invited me back here. When I came, this was really run down, and my co'padre said, 'You take it and fix it.'"

The results looked something like a seven-family yard sale the morning after a windstorm. "They're looking at all kinds of things that maybe they don't see back east," Mike happily explained our obvious curiosity to the kids.

He then proceeded to give us a tour, walking with crutches and dragging his bandaged foot in the muck and straw through the kingdom of the three Mikes.

The only semi-permanent structure was a large tin-roofed shed. Within it was one small room, where the boys sat on a sofa bed playing Nintendo on their TV. Under the same roof there was also a cramped, semi-secluded corridor equipped with a bathtub and a toilet but with no visible plumbing. The rest of the roofed space was open to the elements at the front end and would generally be mistaken for a barn, given the bales of hay, saddles, and halters hanging on a wooden rail. The inadequacy of that conclusion, however, was suggested by the old handleless refrigerator, two full bureaus, and several banks of bright blue gym lockers—Mike called them cubbyholes—each crammed with assorted bits of wire and rope, and unidentifiable scraps of hardware.

Outside—a relative term—things were more expansive. On either side of the shed were the expected features of a roper's home: two well-fenced arenas (with horses in one and half a dozen calves in the other), a homemade horse trailer, and a pickup truck. But the rest of the large grassy lot bore the signs of a remarkably fluid daily life. A line of three sofas under two paloverde trees faced in alternating directions and was surrounded by scattered chairs of every description: metal folding, plastic stacking, seatless wood. Toilets and tubs awaited future service, and a half-dozen cable-spool tables held every manner of jar, can, and tool. The kitchen—composed of a rusting, hand-wrought barbecue smoker (complete with a double-jointed chimney), a formica table, and heaps of pots, pans and utensils—was under the mesquites. Clearly Mike had taken seriously his uncle's admonition that fancy boots don't make a cowboy.

He made his living hauling, or buying and reselling, not just horses but a nearly unlimited range of items. One look around convinced me that Mike had found many of his scavenged treasures too useful to part with. He moved from table to table like a burlesque comedian or magician, fingering the heaps of props, and hence stories, piled on each surface. One table held what looked like a long-handled, rough-hewn crowbar.

"That's a running iron," Mike explained. "See, you can turn the curved top part different ways to make any kind of brand on a cow. It's a cattle rustler's branding iron, because you could carry it with you, and if you came across someone else's calves that were unbranded, or if you wanted to change a brand, you could do it with this. Look how worn the end is. That means it's been used hundreds of times!"

He laughed, leaned over on his crutches, and demonstrated his brand-editing technique in the dirt. On the same table was a can of Tail and Mane shampoo and other horse goods.

"Now, this is great shampoo. We use it for all of us." We laughed along with him.

"Sure," Mike said, more seriously, "lots of things they make for the horse are good for humans, I always dose myself with the cow 'biotics if I get sick."

It was the kind of place some men make when women leave them alone, as I suggested and Mike heartily agreed.

"We couldn't have a woman here. After you get used to it, it's hard to change, because women got to have a mirror for their lipstick and a good light!"

He mimed his hypothetical response. " 'Here's a flashlight.' No, they wouldn't like that!"

Mike warmed to the theme of manly independence.

"Sometimes, like when its cold and you come home real tired after a roping, you might need a bath. But you say, 'Hell, I ain't gonna heat no water tonight. I'll do it tomorrow morning.' "

Mike took us to see his livestock. The roping horses were in one corral, and a smaller pen held some colts.

"This all looks more Indianized," he said, explaining the rough state of the fencing. "It's nothing fancy, but it works. We buy and sell and trade, like the little filly on the other side. I bought her for two hundred and fifty dollars, and I sold her for five hundred. She'll stay here, because I'm boarding her." He eyed the paint with unabashed affection.

"And the sorrel there has a split hoof."

I noted that her corrective shoeing seemed better made than Mike's own.

"Yeah, sometimes I think that his doctor might do me more good than mine!"

Continuing with the inventory, Mike pointed out a young palomino that had come off the White Mountain Apache Reservation.

"They got him with helicopters, and he was so wild that he hit his head real bad. But look at him now. He looks good, and I've already turned down five hundred for him. He had never had a rope on him when we got him. He's quieter now, but he's not a pet yet. See, he's only sixteen months or so, just over a yearling. You break them when they're two or three, but for roping, not til four. You got to bring them into that work little by little, to build up their strength. It's like working in a mine or any hard job. You kind of work up into it. And it's not any good starting earlier, like at two or three. They can't really concentrate til they're four years old. Then they can learn to pay attention. It takes repetition, but if you do too much, they get bored, sulk, and develop bad habits. They are no different from kids. I've had eleven, and I've raised a lot of horses, and I know pretty much how to handle them."

His attention turned from the horses to the boys.

"I'd rather be here than California any day, even if I lived in a tent. And the kids would too. They love it. Back in L.A. they have nothing to do, so they are on the street. Now, when they get home from school at about four, they saddle up and rope maybe two rounds. Little Michael Anthony's mother is back in California, but he wanted to come back to Tucson with me. He doesn't even like to visit there for too long. If his mother asks him to come back, he says, 'No, there's too many ropings here.'"

His grandson, Michael Anthony, concurred.

"It's better here than in L.A. because, I don't know, in the schools out there they won't let you play football. And it's violent. Here it's a little violent, but not like over there. There, it's out of control. I just do better here."

Mike continued.

"They can't get into trouble here. Sure, they can get their finger broken, but I'd rather have them lose a finger than have someone shoot them for drugs. Back in L.A. I built an arena too, but the boys that came around . . . seemed like they were all into drugs. These guys here that come and rope aren't.

"It's real nice for the kids because there's no women involved. If we want to cook up something, we cook up something, or we go over to my niece's to eat, or if we want, we go to the feed store. They play Nintendo, work the horses, whatever they want. The place is rough, the flies are bad in the summer—I gotta put up a screen—but when I say to them that we could get an apartment for about four hundred dollars, they say, 'Nah, that's roping money.'"

Mike laughed at Michael Angel's dedication to the sport.

"All he wants to do is rope. 'What's wrong with you? Ain't you got any interest in girls?' I asked him. He had won a roping with a girl the other day, and they were taking a picture of them together, and I said, 'Hey, she looked pretty good.' But he said, 'I ain't got time for that now. I gotta rope.' He'll go without eating in order to pay some entry fees."

As we talked, little Michael Anthony wrestled his sandals away from one of the three Australian Shepherd dogs, and his young uncle practiced heeling on a simple wooden calf he had put together himself with a sawhorse. The hinged back legs swung when he gave them a whack.

"He's getting where he's pretty good," Mike said, admiring his son's technique. "And the little one, he's getting better. The new system is great for them. All the ropers are given numbers according to their ability. Michael Angel is a three, and the little one is a one, and in any competition there's a number that the two ropers' numbers have to add up to. So if the roping is a five, say, somebody who is a four might rope with Michael Anthony, who's a one. This way the newcomers can get started. And now the higher number guys are beginning to want to rope with the boys."

We all entered the arena to inspect the half dozen roping steers there and the schools of goldfish swimming in the water tank under a ragged saguaro. Mike showed us the plastic horns that ropers now strap on mulies—hornless calves.

"The mulies are cheaper," Mike explained. "If they got good roping horns, they cost fifty or a hundred more, because there are so many people roping. It used to be that they dehorned all their cattle. Now they leave them all."

Meanwhile, the boys demonstrated the prowess of the herd dogs, who ran nipping circles around the frightened calves.

Just then, Mike's co'padre strolled back from the neat brick retirement bungalow he shared with his wife and into the world of the three Mikes.

We all leaned on the pickup while Mike and his old friend conjured up the days of forty years before, when the Old Nogales Highway was a kind of Main Street for cowboys living along it. In those days the Half-Way House—an old-fashioned cowboy bar, restaurant, and dance hall on the side of the old road about halfway between Tucson and Nogales—was a kind of community center, the scene of dances and horse races.

"One time," Mike said, giving us the flavor of those days, "my co'padre here won the jackpot and went into the bar and got pretty well lit. He came home that night with a big steak they had given him for winning, and he showed it to his wife. 'Okay,' she said, 'but where's the horse?'"

"Sure enough," the co'padre laughed, "the horse trailer had broke off some ways back, and I hadn't noticed. I went back to find it. The trailer had rolled over, but nothin' happened to the horse!"

Now the Halfway House stood vacant, the interstate passing it by.

"In them days," Mike said, looking out over the desert and speaking with nostalgia and some consternation for a world gone soft, "the Nogales road went the old way, and Sahuarita was cotton fields. I don't go that much to Mexico now. From what it was, it's just so commercialized. If you go further in, then I'd like to go, to where they still have all the cows in the barn and all the flies around. But I don't like all the little curio shops in Nogales. You used to go there for tequila.

"This new highway," he sighed, "it's nothing like it used to be. Hell, if you got a flat in the old days, you were in trouble. You'd have to fix anything yourself. Now they got twenty-four-hour call and things like that. All these call boxes . . . there weren't no call boxes! If you ran out of gas, that was your fault."

By the closed border crossing of Lochiel, Arizona

green valleys

One is struck by the green of the golf courses. A flash of color between dry, brown hills just west of the interstate about twenty-five miles south of Tucson. Beyond, there are others, each a brilliant, gently rolling carpet surrounded by tidy rows of brick and stucco houses clustered according to size. The green of Green Valley was not a miner's delusion but a developer's prophecy.

As strangely out of place as this landscape may seem here, in one sense it is but the latest phase of what Thomas Sheridan, in his book *Arizona: A History,* calls the transformation stage in Arizona's political ecology: an aggressive submission of the environment to human will rather than the other way around.

Every crop got started subtly somewhere in the world where it made sense, often as little more than human encouragement of what was already going on. As people wanted more food or found themselves in places less fit for the enterprise, they had to do more to make things grow—plow, fertilize, even carry, pump, or divert water to their crops.

That sort of agriculture arrived here in the 1950s, when the Farmer's Investment Company (FICO) left California for the cheaper lands of southern Arizona. FICO bought up much of the Santa Cruz valley, planting cotton first and then, beginning in the 1960s, another southeastern transplant: pecan trees. Now the largest pecan orchard in the United States stretches for miles along the dry riverbed—six thousand acres of neatly rowed nut trees beginning just north of Sahuarita, where there is a large processing plant and tourist shop. The Feedlot Cafe in Continental is all that remains of another FICO enterprise: a cattle-feeding station that in its heyday fed 40,000 head at a time.

That form of agriculture gave way, in a sense, to the golf courses. By the 1970s the citizens of Green Valley (FICO had sold the land for their community to developers) had concluded that the feedlot was "incompatible with their lifestyle." FICO acquiesced.

So golf courses are part of the transformation stage. Better suited for wetter climes, they have spread throughout the world, the grass a never-harvested money crop. They have come even to the desert, where the weather is conducive to the game if not to the playing field. No doubt future archaeologists will enjoy tracing their distribution and arguing about the reasons for such apparently irrational land use around the world. They will find clues in the traces of nearby human settlements and learn to distinguish those in which golf courses were more or less peripheral from those where that sacred landscape occupied the geographic and social center, the very raison d'être of the place. We call such peculiar settlements resorts and retirement communities.

Resorts offer only a brief pause in the cycle of birth, work, and death, but the retirement communities are party to a permanent defiance of both human and natural order. They are, in a way, an assertion of the possibility of complete control, vigilantly excluding youth and the appearance of either growth or decay and alleging eternal, healthy seniorhood. No birth. No death.

Green Valley, the brilliant oasis that straddles the interstate here, is such a place, carved into the body of what had been the great Canoa Ranch. Millions of gallons of pumped water and the American passion for orderly and highly organized leisure have created this world. The inhabitants, when they are not power walking in sun visors and silver hair, circulate in golf carts—not just on the courses but through the streets and malls as well.

Eleanor Smith's home was in one of the dozens of housing estates that comprise this sprawling retirement community. The looping caminos, calles, and paseos of her neighborhood, La Cañada, no doubt make sense from the air. On the ground they are more than a little disorienting to the uninitiated. After the third pass around the same ornamental cactus garden island in the road, I finally picked the right paseo and found her simple white rectangular bungalow.

Eleanor was as well groomed as her raked-earth cactus garden, but she was not what I had come to expect in a Green Valley woman—no jogging suit or electric green slacks. She was a tall, slowly graceful, delicate bird, an old-fashioned southern lady from Missouri in a flowered dress.

Like many Americans, Eleanor introduced herself by means of a house tour, as if to say, "This is what I made. This is how I live. This is who I am." Though her home was as immaculate as Eleanor herself, it was more unrelentingly modern than I had expected. The large, airy living room through which we passed had none of the memorabilia—family photos and such—that should have been there. Instead, the nearly stark space was dominated by her daughter's large abstract canvases. They added color and some small movement but did nothing to threaten the calm, clean order of the room. In any case, Eleanor devoted most of her tour to the small "office" she had consecrated to a high-end PC and printer.

"This is where I do my computer work."

Eleanor smiled, and with some intensity booted up her machine and flipped through screen after screen of stock listings and calculations. Next to the computer was a neat stack of printouts.

"I am keeping track of my family's investments," she explained. "It takes me several hours a day."

Having returned to the cool comfort of the living room, I asked Eleanor to tell me about life in Green Valley.

"There are others who would be better suited to give you an account of the political organization or the history of the community. As for me, I came here as a widow in 1982 because a good friend of mine had moved here. I guess it was a place for widows. There are all kinds of activities for people like me. It's a wonderful place, really. You have to join the Recreation Association, and the dues are $245 a year. There are four huge centers with pools, shops, jewelry stores, movies, dances. There are nine pools, in fact, and many planned activities. And of course there's everything you need, churches and banks.

"But I chose to do nothing. I did work as a secretary for the home-owners association for this neighborhood for eleven years, but I stopped a few months ago. Do you see, I have no time. I have to keep up with my computer work."

It seemed a strange compulsion at the age of seventy-three, a useful pastime that had somehow become an all-absorbing obsession, drawing Eleanor inward and away from her neighbors—but also, perhaps, away from the past. I had often been in the homes of such southern ladies, and I could not help noticing, once again, the strange scarcity of relics: photos, odd chairs, and occasional tables.

There were also few material traces of the region. What had this world to do with the world beyond it, I wondered, the desert, and Mexico only forty miles south?

"Do you go to Mexico at all?" I asked.

"I went last year for the first time in over ten years," she answered, "on a mission tour. A friend of mine had called me up and asked would I go along on this tour, to see the missions of Sonora. I said I didn't want to go, that I would never go back to that country or ever leave the United States again. But she talked me into it, and I had a wonderful time. Our tour leader did a wonderful job, taking us to all the missions and telling us everything about them."

Her face had changed utterly, her tiny, thin cheeks pinching inward, when she said that she would never go south of the border again. I asked why.

"Well," she began, "that is a story. You see, my husband, Smitty, and I used to go down there all the time—to Mexico. My husband was an engineer. He retired from Fort Huachuca in 1976. We had roamed all around Mexico before that, and we talked a lot about retiring there. So we went down in our RV to explore the possibilities. Our first thought was that maybe we'd retire in Oaxaca. We liked the Indian culture. My husband collected artifacts—crafts, pots, baskets—and he liked the Indians there. So we started trying to buy a piece of land in Oaxaca. You see, my husband was a Missouri farm boy, and he wasn't going to be happy with some little plot of land and a house. He wanted to farm, to raise some cattle. "Well, we fooled around with attorneys for a couple of years, but Echeverría, the president then, didn't want foreigners to buy land. Little bits maybe, but we wanted a real ranch, enough to raise cattle.

"Well, we met a group of American youngsters—nomads, you'd call them— in a van down there. They had been traveling all over, and we asked them where they would go to look for land like that. They all said Guatemala. They said it was politically stable, beautiful, and that we could buy land there with no problem. So we decided that's where we'd go.

"We stored everything, got into our RV, and headed for Cobán in the mountains of Guatemala. It was really beautiful. The climate was good up in the mountains. Mists would sweep along. We found some property in a cloud forest on the side of a mountain. Standing on the land, you could see all the way to Mexico, a whole world before you. And there was no problem buying the land, so we started construction right away. You see, Smitty had lots of energy, drive, and intelligence. He was determined to build the house, so he went to Guatemala City and hired Indians. He taught them to build and he supervised them.

"Well, Smitty was having a wonderful time building a house and warehouse.

It was architecturally lovely, set on three hundred acres on the side of the mountain. We had been there about two months, and a friend of ours, Terry, was down for a while from West Virginia to help with the house. He was an excellent cabinetmaker, and he had come to do all the woodwork for us. He had ordered ten thousand board feet of mahogany shipped to us there.

"It was a Saturday morning, and Terry and Smitty were up on the mountain at the building site with the Indians, and I was down picking asparagus in the garden. You see, Smitty had built a beautiful little temporary house surrounded by a cane fence, and that's where I had put a little garden. Well, there I was in the garden when about fifteen guerrillas suddenly just stormed in through the cane gate. About half of them came to me there—they were heavily armed—and the others went up to where Smitty was. They put me at gunpoint and went into the house. Well, they just wrecked everything, and they came out with the Indian gatekeeper.

"Now, all this time Smitty was up with Terry. I sat there and heard the gunshots on the mountain. I thought, This isn't kid stuff going on up there.

"Meanwhile, the ones down at the little house were breaking all the dishes and yelling 'Pollos!' Chickens! We had just brought them back from town. Then the other group came down from the mountain, bringing our friend Terry with them at gunpoint. " 'Eleanor,' he said to me, 'they want guns and money. Give them what they want. It's a matter of life and death.'

"Well, I didn't know where the guns were. 'Smitty knows,' I said.

" 'Smitty is dead,' Terry said.

"They set fire to the little house. Then they asked for gasoline to start our car on fire. They tried to burn it, but they couldn't keep the fire going. Then their leader came over to us—they had us kneeling on the ground—and he delivered a whole spiel, that it was all 'Por los pobres,' that they were an army of the poor and that we were *mierda,* shit. They hated Americans. 'If you or any of your other Americans come here, . . .'

"Just then an army helicopter arrived above us, just that split second. Otherwise I'm sure they would have shot us in the back. I was told that the Spanish tradition is to never take prisoners. God was up there doing something for us. Not for Smitty, though.

"The helicopter fired a machine gun, and they all split to take cover like rabbits, and Terry and I ran onto the road. Terry ran up ahead and hid. I found a place by a barbed-wire fence and took off the bright yellow sweater I was wearing.

"I had a will to live and yet a willingness to die. I was just as cool as a cucumber. A state of shock, I guess, like a robot. I heard a truck, then I heard voices, clinking belts. Some men were talking, and then they left. When it was dark, Terry came up to where I was, and the two of us walked through the night to the village. There was a gypsum mine out there, and there were trucks passing on their way there, but no one would pick us up. So we walked two or three miles to where we knew some Guatemalan friends who had a sawmill.

"When we got to the mill, it was in ashes. There were Guatemalan army trucks and soldiers there by the burned sawmill, and I went up to them and told them that guerrillas had killed my husband and burned our house. The soldiers took us back to our house and up the mountain to where Smitty lay dead. They got him moved out of the sun. I started talking to Terry about what to do next. 'Eleanor,' he said to me, 'You are not planning to stay here!'

"A little Guatemalan truck was there to take Smitty back to Cobán. We drove out that night, and we stopped to tell another American friend what had happened. Later on, we got to the road for Cobán and all of a sudden the little truck with Smitty in the back of it passed in front of us.

"That was the last time I saw him, his big feet sticking out of the little truck. I didn't want to see Smitty again there. A few days later I borrowed some black clothes to go to the funeral."

A dancer arranges her coiffure before taking the stage at the Fiesta de Tumacacori

ranches and relics

With a twist of her long walking stick, Barb Ruppman pulled aside a low scraggle of creosote.

"Look," she told us, "that's the old camino right through there."

Our eyes followed her gesture. An unremarkable space, a stream of weeds and buffelgrass between the higher mesquite and cottonwoods, took shape before us, the ghost of a road, the 250-year-old way to Mexico. On either side, as Barb pointed out, were the fragments of lives lived along it since that time, from nails to house foundations.

The road and the houses were in fact clearly marked on the simple map she held in her hands, a copy of the eighteenth-century original that was hanging only a hundred yards away, just inside the entrance to Tubac's Presidio Museum.

Founded in 1752 in response to an O'odham revolt, the Tubac presidio was the northernmost outpost of New Spain. When Hugh O'Conor arrived there in 1775, Juan Bautista de Anza had departed for San Francisco Bay, leaving behind a few dispirited troops. O'Conor moved the garrison to Tucson. The map shows that the soldiers had not lived within ramparts but in a small village of individually fortified houses. The captain's home was a bit larger and had a walled courtyard like that of a medieval manor house, large enough to shelter the people in case of attack. The several dozen other, more modest structures and a cemetery were loosely clustered around the life-giving river. The colonists had created a football-shaped fertile parcel divided into fields with the help of an irrigation ditch that left and then rejoined the Santa Cruz River.

Roads, too, appear on the map, as faint lines tentatively leading off through the wilderness to the south, west, and east, and straighter and more certainly to the north. They are labeled boldly enough: El Camino de Tumacacori, del Altar, de Sonoitac, de San Xavier del Bac.

None of these trails have survived as roads. We were looking at, trying to imagine, the road to Mexico: El Camino de Tumacacori on the map. Like a river shifting its bed, the road has moved steadily west over the years. Replacing the trail, the Old Nogales Highway remained unpaved until the early years of this century. It ran through the middle of the village of Tubac, passed by the cemetery, and continued south through what is now a mesquite forest. Then, in the late 1950s, a new and straighter road was built just to the west of the village. Frontage Road, as it is now called, appears and disappears at various points between Tucson and Nogales. Only the interstate, just west again, makes the whole trip to Mexico.

The town has suffered more vicissitudes than the road. Silver mines attracted many adventurers over the years, and the relatively well watered and fertile valley supported farms and cattle. But the Apache raids made life dangerous and, after 1821, nearly impossible. Mexican independence left the national treasury depleted, and the "peace payments" with which the Apaches had been placated ceased. Attacks became more frequent and deadly. The town dwindled and was abandoned more than once, to be revived in more secure times and under American rule. In the last decades of the nineteenth century, Tubac sat amidst the large ranches and small homesteads of cattle country. Most of the homesteads were Mexican, settled by people like Mike Murat's great-grandfather.

Now times have changed again. There are still many Mexican American people living in Tubac and in the nearby communities of Tumacacori and Carmen. But their presence is not apparent in any public space, except perhaps in the cemetery, most of whose gravestones bear Spanish names. Local real estate is expensive now and is sought by a new breed of permanent or seasonal migrants called snowbirds (retirees and others who come down from the Midwest and elsewhere to enjoy southern Arizona's mild winters).

The contemporary village of Tubac is described as an art colony, which seems to mean here, as elsewhere, that there's a lot of arty pottery for sale. Tourists come here looking for it and for the more traditional Mexican pots, *santos* (statues of saints) and *chimeneas* (small, freestanding pottery fireplaces). History too has been packaged for public consumption and can now be found in the museum. But the old town and the old trails and roads—even the colonial caminos—have not really disappeared; they are just a bit harder to see, which is why we went to look for them with Barbara Ruppman.

You might easily mistake Barb for one of the tourists or snowbirds. A slim, pretty blonde who seems far younger than her years, in white slacks and pastel windbreaker she looks and sounds like the Minnesotan she is. But Barb is happier in the bush than in the shops, and far more excited by a shard of dull red Indian earthenware kicked up from the dirt by a passing horse than by a signed polychromatic fruit bowl. She came here nine years ago with her house-building husband for the climate, but she was equally drawn here by the area's exotic history, a past that was not her own. A childhood fascination with arrowheads has flowered into a nearly full-time avocation as an archaeologist.

In this pursuit Barb has two vital assets: great eyes and an historical imagination. The eyes see two millimeters of rusting iron at thirty paces. Her imagination sees a house where there is only a dotted line of weed-covered foundation stones and, more remarkably, conjures human pain from burnt and shattered clay.

"These are house foundations," she said, dragging the end of the walking stick over some rocks sticking up through the crusted earth. "There were soldiers' houses all through here. And this one," she said, stepping into a shallow excavation in one of the foundations, "is really amazing. You can see that there were at least four different houses here, one after the other." She traced tiers of stone, each at a slightly different angle, each some inches above the next.

"And this is where I found a pot. It was broken but all there, and charred black on the top rim. I remember picking it up and saying, 'This wasn't thrown away. It broke right where I found it, in the house, never moved. And the charring . . .'

"I looked at the woman I was working with, and we talked about what might have happened: a burning roof collapsing, an Indian raid. Of course, we don't know, but we like to imagine the lives of these people, their fears and hopes."

Taking us to her home, Barb showed us her own collection of artifacts, the only relative eccentricity there. It was, like all personal museums, an idiosyncratic assemblage, ranging in her case from polished fossils to Indian pots, gleaned as often as not from garage sales. There was nothing from Minnesota in the collection.

Her most prized discovery did come from her dig in Tubac: a tiny silver religious medal, with the crucifixion pictured on one face and a Madonna on the other.

"This was a real thrill, it is so beautiful. This is a copy I had made. The original is in the museum."

The museum, in fact, contains a great and fascinating array of artifacts, from Hohokam Indian pottery at least six hundred years old to fragments of the often tragically interrupted colonists' lives from the last two centuries. Their history is now "our" history, contained and ordered in a state park where the chronological sequence of technology implies, as always, struggle and progress.

But there are also the more apparently disconnected fragments of domestic lives. Some of these no doubt seem exotic to most visitors, but some must be hauntingly familiar—or both, like the religious medal Barb found or the wall of *retablos*.

Small, naive paintings on tin and wood, retablos depict personal moments of calamity over two centuries: a horse, startled by an armadillo, throws its rider; a fire claims a rustic cabin; a difficult childbirth nearly takes a young mother's life. In each case disaster was averted, as the grateful written account typically incorporated into the piece recounts, on a given date, through the divine intervention of the figure shown floating in a cloud in the upper righthand corner of the picture. In fact, that holy personage—Christ, Mary, or a saint—is shown not in his or her living form but as the statue or image known to the artist and devotee.

The practice of painting retablos, a Spanish custom the Tubac settlers brought with them, is an intriguing feature of Mediterranean popular Catholicism. More, perhaps, than any other Western devotional expression, it uses the power of art to bind person, community, and divinity. A retablo is an intimate portrait, a private event and a memory rendered permanent, protected from the vagaries of time by expression in color and line. But retablos are not kept at home, still less in museums. Normally they are brought to churches and shrines and placed near the representation of the sacred person credited with the miracle—a statue, an icon, or a relic. In this way the painting, typically the work of a local artist, becomes part of a collective work of art and faith, a collage of human misfortune. They are also, of course, a testimonial to the power of the saint or virgin whose image they surround. The more miracles, the more retablos; the more retablos, the more prayers; the more prayers, the more miracles.

Jean England Neubauer also lives with artifacts. In her case, however, the history they contain is her own family's. While a few of these objects are arranged in a tiny exhibit in the Santa Cruz Chili Factory, most of these secular relics have been given the run of her homes. Saddles, paintings, scrapbooks, photos, furniture— every piece has a family narrative attached.

Meeting Jean outside of her domestic setting, however, one would not suspect that she is so rooted in the past. She met us at the Chili Factory, just a couple of miles south of Tubac on the Frontage Road. A bright-eyed, attractive blonde, Jean wore jeans and moved and spoke casually with her employees, most of them Mexican American natives of the immediate area.

She gave us a brief tour of the mementos arranged outside the office there, including fabulous photos of her family ranch in Sonora, famous cowboy movie star relations, and fields of chiles. But Jean is a businesswoman—a banker for a number of years and still on the board of a Tucson bank. She settled behind a massive oak desk, her eyes dancing with enthusiasm as she spoke less of the past than of the present and future, getting excited over numbers, increased efficiency, new products, risks, and, hopefully, profits.

But at the Rock Corral Ranch, her childhood home in nearby Tumacacori, her mood changed. There, she was on and of the land and was perhaps more connected to her locally famous mother. Judy England was loved throughout the region, and her recently departed spirit was everywhere around us in the house. It was she who had filled the house with the memorabilia of her own family, from the original immigrant from England, whose invention of the McClellan saddle made him a Civil War fortune, to the Washington socialite Aunt Bessie, whose ornate black-lace fan was framed over a bed, and her improvident nephew, Jean's grandfather John, who went west.

We looked with amusement at his carefully arranged and preserved Harvard scrapbook, the highlights of which were press clippings of a series of mild outrages, culminating in his dismissal from those hallowed halls. He was clearly a charming and lovable rake. Convinced that a radical change of venue was in order, Aunt Bessie sent him packing off to the distant desert to work with a relative who was mapping the border region of Sonora. He liked it well enough to buy a ranch near Magdalena de Kino in Sonora, where he built a sprawling fortress of a home furnished with massive Victoriana sent west by Aunt Bessie.

"I think she felt it would ensure a civilized life," Jean said, laughing.

Throughout her childhood, Jean took trips to the Mexican ranch, even after it was sold. "We'd go there and picnic on the land," she told us. "But now we don't go down anymore. It's gotten a bit dangerous in that area."

Aunt Bessie's civilized furnishings followed Jean to her homes in Tucson and Tumacacori, joining the other family memorabilia.

"Dad bought this ranch in the thirties and built this home."

We had settled down in a cool stone room, where Jean began to speak, with great affection, about ranching. She was hardly romantic about it—she is annoyed by people who mistake animals for people—but her sense of her own and others' connection with the land still filled her with wonder.

She laughed when I asked about how many head of cattle she had.

"Around here, you never ask how many acres or how many head of cattle someone has. It's like asking how much you make a year back east, or how much is in your bank account.

"You need at least three hundred head to be viable," she explained, "and then you only make twenty thousand a year. We don't have that here. I guess we are lucky to break even."

Jean grazes her modest herd of cattle on her own range and on about ten thousand acres of national forest land. The Forest Service's long-term, low-payment leasing arrangement is the basis of ranching in the West. In the words of Thomas Sheridan, behind every rugged individualist there's a government agency.

I asked her about her position in the often bitter disputes over this form of public land use. In the latest chapter of the continuing western saga of the range wars, it was ranchers versus ecologists and the park rangers who tried to enforce federal legislation limiting the use of what ranchers had come to regard as their private property. Ranchers often talked like they themselves would soon join the stickleback guppy on the endangered species list, invoking the cowboy way of life as more precious and more threatened than any amphibian losing his niche to buffelgrass.

"The thing you have to understand about ranching here is that there is a big difference between a small family farm or ranch like this one, with long-term interests in the place, versus large companies that may be looking for a short-term profit or tax write-off. The small rancher is going to look after the public lands he uses, because he wants to continue there for generations. And the cattle rotation there is good for the land. It invigorates growth.

"You see, in local ranching families there is a continuity of knowledge, not only with the ranchers but with the hands. Some of the ranch hands here can count generations of family at Rock Corral. One of them knew far more about the chiltepine pepper, which is growing wild here, than any botanist."

Talk of big ranches reminded me of Ray Denton, the gentle, soft-spoken manager of a large cattle company near Arivaca, where more than eight hundred head roamed over about 120,000 acres—188 square miles—only 20,000 of which belonged to the cattle company. The remaining land belonged to the government and was administered by the Bureau of Land Management.

Whether the cattle company had long-term interests I could not say. Indeed, the present owners, Ray told us, rarely visited the place. But Ray himself was as much a part of the local landscape as it is possible to be.

We had come across the ranch one morning, having turned right in downtown Amado—home of the famous cow skull building, a post office-cum-junk shop, and the Cow Palace restaurant—and traveled west a few miles into the hilly grasslands. Inside the gate was a corral draped with saddles and blankets, and with a few horses already looking for shade. Above, clusters of burlap feedbags looked like large tobacco leaves. We walked up to a group of Mexican American ranch

Vaqueros on a cigarette break in Arivaca Junction, Arizona

hands who were emerging from the screened porch behind the ranch house, gripping their enamel mugs of coffee. Ray came out with them, and when asked if he minded photographs, he said, "Sure, go ahead," and invited us to take a truck ride with him to check on some young bulls.

"This time of the year we are mostly repairing fences—hundreds of miles of them," he told us as he nudged his truck into gear and rolled out over the dirt road.

"And raising colts. Most of the work is still done on horseback here. We break them in the washes. The sand slows them down."

I wondered whether it was all business, or did they "rope" like the three Mikes.

"Oh yeah, everybody here ropes. Me too. I like the new number system. It's good for people like me," he said, smiling with self-deprecation, "because now I get a chance to compete. I even won a belt myself in a rancher's competition one year.

"But these horses are for work. We are still riding the range, and the big moment is the cattle roundup in October."

I asked him where the cattle went when they left the ranch.

"We sold the cattle to a broker. That's the way it works now. He would already have his buyers, but where they finally end up I couldn't tell you."

At Ray's signal I hopped out and unlatched a wooden gate. He drove the truck into the fenced field, got out, and led us to a group of young bulls hidden under a stand of mesquite. In the next field four steers grazed under a cottonwood.

"Those over there are my own," Ray told us, reminding me of what was so easy to forget: that the hundreds of other head did not belong to him but to a distant owner. He explained that he liked to have a few head of his own, and I asked why.

"That I couldn't tell you," he said, smiling with just a hint of self-mockery. "I guess there's no good reason, but I like to have them just the same."

Meanwhile, the young bulls before us took no more notice of our presence than of the coyote trotting through the scrub on the other side of the fence. Danny surveyed his realm.

"We're lucky. There's a good water supply here. Ours comes from the west—drains that way—while just a bit further north, like at the Canoa Ranch, the level has dropped considerably, because of the mines' use of water up that way. Still, we are dependent on the rain. We did really well for a few years in a row, but last year there wasn't much rain. That hurt us."

Squinting over the mesquite brush and buffelgrass, he continued, "If you abuse it you won't have it. Of course, there are some, . . . but most people, you'll find, are careful with the land.

"But you look at the reserve," he said, referring to the newly created Buenos Aires National Wildlife Refuge, whose thousands of acres had once been part of a huge ranch reaching to the Mexican border. "I'm not sure they always know what they're doing."

It was, I thought, not just a question of different economic or ecological perspectives. Ray clearly felt that park rangers and others like them may have a kind of generalized knowledge, but general knowledge did not always work well in a particular landscape. For him, landscapes were like people, each one different. Intimate knowledge was only to be had by living on and in it. Ray's father had come from cattle country farther north to manage the ranch forty-one years earlier. Ray had been a small boy at the time.

"I guess I learned about the ranch by growing up on it that way," he said, "and about other things in the one-room schoolhouse that was there then. I'd say about sixty percent of the kids were Mexican, so we all grew up speaking both English and Spanish. Some of the hands there went to school with me. They grew up, and still live, on the ranch."

We asked him, growing up as he did, surrounded by the two languages and cultures, whether he often went to Mexico.

"I love to go there, but I don't much linger in Nogales, on the border. The towns don't interest me. But I love to get in my truck and go to Puerto Lobos to fish. Or head into the hills of Chihuahua. That's real ranch country. I'll just stop at some place there and talk with the people about ranches and the life and conditions there. They're great people.

"But the border near the ranch here," he continued, looking south over the hills, "that's another thing altogether. Drugs. I coulda got myself in a real jam just a few years ago. It was late in the evening and we had just finished branding, and I heard a truck off in a big sand wash not too far from the road, and I told the guys, 'Go on ahead into camp. I'm gonna see if I can help those people.' I thought they were hunters or weekend warriors. Well I went down there and like a fool—I wasn't thinkin'—I went in and walked around, and I didn't see anybody around the truck, and I walked over to it and it had a tarp on it. I raised up the tarp and here were all these little packages, and I felt the hair stand up on my neck. I realized that them boys musta been watching me—probably had a rifle trained on me right that moment. Well, I got the hell away from that thing.

"I called the Border Patrol on that one. There for a while, the folks over there—the Border Patrol—got so tough on the trucks that they started backpackin' it. Ten or twelve guys with backpacks, just walkin' across."

In speaking of the history of her own ranch, Jean Neubauer naturally talked of her father. He too had combined a love of the land with the spirit of a restless entrepreneur.

"My father had more free time, like all cowboys when the screwworm problem was solved in the late 1930s by releasing sterile flies. They used to have to ride the range constantly, doctoring steers, but now they had free time.

"Well, he had land in Amado that had been used for Pima cotton, and he thought it would be good for raising chiles. He was right. You see, he had something in mind. He wanted to use his own chiles to get pure chile powder—nobody else was doing that—and then he invented an apparatus for squeezing chiles and getting a pure paste."

We knew the paste well, with its deep, intense flavor and color. No wonder it was and continues to be a great success, selling well enough that the company grew up around it.

Jean must have inherited her entrepreneurial spirit from her father, but it seems as though it's been in the family a long time, and on both sides.

Besides the family mementos there on the Rock Corral Ranch, there were artifacts of a more local origin. One was a useful piece of local folk art—a small santo.

"That," Jean told us, "is San Isidro. People here believe that he can bring rain, and they will pray to him if the rains don't come when they should."

She laughed quietly. "My father—even though he was an Episcopalian—built a shrine for him out in the back because the ranch hands and their families believed so strongly in him. But if he doesn't do his job, if the rains don't come as they should, you might find him hanging upside down in the elderberry tree!"

But San Isidro, whose power was needed to maintain the cycle of the seasons, was now on a mantel, out of context like the other saints pictured on the retablos in the Tubac museum. After all their travels, they had at least found one another again, even if not in a church.

But the saints will outlive the museums, public and private. The sense that all museums give of having finally contained, ordered, and even ended history is an illusion.

The mission at Tumacacori is now a museum as well, or rather a national monument, prefaced by a museum through which the visitor passes on the way

Mission wall and bell tower, Tumacacori National Monument

into the mission itself. Masses are occasionally celebrated in the mission ruins, and there are still Indian graves—modest, elongated piles of stones and white crosses—just outside its walls, seeming to resist inclusion in the exhibit. They are really there, in that earth, and nothing written about them or positioned around them can make them into artifacts.

Avenida Obregón, Nogales, Sonora

crossing

"There is no border!" The announcer's voice was taut with emotion as he shouted to the crowd assembled for the Fiesta de Tumacacori.

Maybe so, from an announcer's or a folklorist's perspective, but others are inclined to see the matter differently, like Doris Meissner, commissioner of the Immigration and Naturalization Service, and Dutch Steenbakker, assistant chief Border Patrol agent. They were busy in the Coronado National Forest six miles from Nogales and the border. The peso had crashed, and although the insurgency in Chiapas had apparently been quieted, there were revelations of deepening corruption in the Mexican federal government. In preparation for "the unlikely event of an immigrant stampede" immigration officials—with the help of the U.S. Army—held field exercises, practicing the capture, detention, and relocation of masses of simulated illegal immigrants. Mexican government officials, not surprisingly, were less than happy with this display of neighborly concern, but Meissner and company were having far too good a time with their role-playing to stop.

"Planning makes the difference between an effective response and just dissembling," she said.

Not that the U.S. government has anything like a consistent attitude toward the border. The Department of Transportation talks, like the folklorist, about the "invisible borders" of NAFTA and the facilitation of truck transport in both directions. In fact, the heaviest use of the interstate is by truckers bringing Mexican-grown fruit and vegetables across the line and up to a group of produce companies about twenty miles north in Rio Rico.

But our government's capitalist concern with the free flow of commodities is balanced—or undermined—by a sporadic desire, usually in response to a political campaign, to prevent other sorts of free-market flow: undocumented workers and drugs. So, even as the Department of Transportation reduces border red tape for Mexican truckers (though some are turned back when they show up at the checkpoint with orange crates in place of driver's seats), the customs officials are urged to stop more of the drug traffic, and the Border Patrol plays war games in the national forest.

One's sense of the border depends on how he or she looks at it. The experience of "crossing" changes with time and place, and with the company one keeps.

We took the "truck route" across the border, Mariposa Road, which enters Mexico on the eastern edge of Nogales. Immediately after crossing, we turned off to the west and, passing a couple of new-looking factory buildings, descended abruptly into Nogales's largest cemetery, El Panteón Nacional. To our left and right, hills of graves rose to the horizon, and around, between, and on them strolled, labored, lunched, and chatted hundreds of people.

It was the first of November, the last day of preparations for El Día de los Muertos—the Day of the Dead—a distinctly Mexican occasion and not at all the tourist attraction in Nogales that it is much farther south. Elsewhere, the light of the candles on the graves is washed out by a circle of powerful lamps that enable the gringos to videotape the cemetery vigil through the night.

Not so in Nogales. The locals were preparing their families' grave sites—cleaning and watering them, painting, recarpeting, placing flowers, and giving them myriad other attentions and adornments.

For these tasks, all that was necessary was at hand; an entire Mexican village had sprung up around the perimeter of the cemetery. Along the fences on both sides of the road, a dozen pickup trucks were parked, their sides extended upward by oddments of plywood, each of them loaded with a glowing orange-gold heap of thousands of marigolds: the preferred flower for the dead. More permanent structures had also been erected, the kind of slapped and nailed together random plank and scrap stands that surround every Mexican fiesta. Here they were selling flowers, flower crosses, and plastic and living decorations of every description and dimension for the graves. At the eastern gates of the cemetery there were no less than two dozen makeshift cantinas serving the usual run of tacos and tamales, as well as the pot and blanket salesmen who seem to appear along the outer edge of every fiesta. Also typical is the photographer strolling among the lunchers, offering a Polaroid memorial of the day of memory.

To see such a dizzying array of activity around a cemetery is, for most Americans, unreal enough, but perhaps the most striking and unexpected thing about the Day of the Dead is the presence, even the dominance, of children. They are everywhere, nibbling snacks on their grandparents' graves, running singly and more often in packs, buying cotton candy and balloons from the peddlers that stroll among the tombs, delightedly mugging for our cameras, and earning pesos by cleaning graves.

Two such boys, each about twelve years old, found unexpected employment burying the dead.

Before another cemetery gate, flanked by a balloon salesman and a marigold truck, a poor man stood theatrically still, holding before him a tiny coffin entirely covered in what appeared to be white fake fur. Around him, in distracted silence, a group of equally ragged children and adults watched and waited for his next move. So did the vendors, grave cleaners, and I, my own outsider's curiosity matched by that of the locals, many of whom stared brazenly at the man, obviously but only casually interested in the drama unfolding before them.

Suddenly the man's head—hitherto erect and stoic—fell forward onto the little coffin and he began to sob, silently but forcefully. After a long moment, he turned toward the open gate and proceeded into the cemetery, his contingent of mourners and a few of the curious following behind. A narrow, winding trail between the tombstones led to the upper edge of the cemetery and a very modest grave already home to an older relation.

Without the aid of a priest, the man laid his infant to rest in the shallow grave dug by the young boys he had hired for the purpose. The father, as he must have been, was no longer weeping. Rigid with enormous sadness, he sprinkled water from a can with his hand, making the sign of the cross on the fresh earth, while two young girls watched, draped over the little wooden cross like Currier and Ives angels.

Christmas Eve in Nogales. We have come to watch people shop on both sides of the border: the Americans who seek curios on Avenida Obregón and the Mexicans who come for all manner of goods to Morley Street—La Morley—one of several parallel roads that run up against the border.

The automobile traffic is on Grand Street, funneled through the large customs gates of both countries. Immediately to the east are the railroad tracks that run up against a great rusting barrier, part of the combination of high chain-link fence and sheets of corrugated metal that attempts to realize the concept of "the nation."

The impeded railroad makes one think of Europe, where even the Iron Curtain rarely materialized so literally and where today the traveler crosses every manner of international border, sometimes awakened on trains by officials armed with the stamps of old and brand-new nations but allowed to continue east or west. The border between France and Germany—defined and redefined in book and horror over the last century—is no impediment. But France and Germany are members of the European Union, and whatever NAFTA means economically, it clearly does not mean "community" in any human sense of the word. If the French and Germans see one another as fellow Europeans, Americans and Mexicans do not—could not, here at this border—see one another as fellow North Americans.

The American dialectic of race and ethnicity is different, especially at the edge. This border has no room for ambiguity and relativity. You are either one thing or the other. The American customs officials sort racially. They are absolutely consistent. If you look Mexican, you must show the requisite identification: a card that proves your citizenship or permission to stay in or visit the United States. If you do not look Mexican, and most especially if you are blond and confused and laden with tourist trinkets, you will be asked the rhetorical question "American?" or "U.S. citizen?" and waved through. No papers needed; your face is your passport.

America is defined at this verge not by its average person but by its iconic self-image.

A beautiful young woman is stopped by a customs official. She looks like many Mexican women of her generation on both sides of the divide: tight jeans; long, crimped black hair cascading over and around large gold loop earrings; shocking pink lipstick; and constantly animated, nearly black eyes. Her skin is very white. Apparently she does not have the right papers, because I hear her explain in heavily accented but capable English that she was born in Los Angeles General Hospital. The customs officer, speaking with a New York accent and idiom, claims ignorance of any such hospital, noting that he lived for years in that city.

"I am not accusing you of anything, understand," he tells her, "but I have to warn you that if you say you are a U.S. citizen and you're not, if you lie, it's a felony and you will be subject to arrest."

He delivers these lines in a way that is not menacing but that does seek to communicate two points: that he is doing his job and that he is not calling her a name. She is frustrated but cooperative, as is the young man behind her in line, who turns out to be her husband. They are told to wait inside the small booth that serves here, at the Morley Street crossing, to house the U.S. Customs office.

The booth interrupts the fence that runs east along International Street about a hundred yards and then mounts one of the many steep hills that so define the landscape of the two cities named Nogales. On the hill, the fence separates a slum, or *colonia,* of shacks, goats, chickens, and laundry in Mexico from a grassy knoll on the American side.

The Mexican side is animated. While we watch, a man's head pops up over the high fence about a hundred feet east of the little customs booth. He looks down and around quickly and signals up the line with a wave of his hand. A bit farther up the hill, only a hundred yards or so from where the young woman claiming to be from Los Angeles is awaiting due process, another fence watcher stares through the chain-link fence into America. He pulls a snipped flap of wire fence aside while a man and a woman climb briskly through to the United States. The man clambers down the hill and slides over a sheet of corrugated metal onto International Street. He takes off his jacket and wraps it around his meager belongings, ducks behind a truck to gather his wits, and then strides off to the north. The woman behind him hesitates on the grass and then changes her mind and reenters Mexico. Every few minutes, another pilgrim steps through the barrier, always within plain sight of any official who cares to look over his or her shoulder. But they do not look.

"You want the truth?" the customs officer says, answering my query about the irony of the process. "Sure, it's a waste of taxpayers' dollars, but if they didn't waste it here, they'd spend it on weapons systems that don't work. One way or another they are gonna waste it. I know they're crossing through the fence up there, but I am doing my job. This is what I'm paid to do. What kills me is when they try to cross here, through the gate, and they claim to be U.S. citizens and they're not. It's a felony, and we have to arrest them, when all they have to do is cross a few feet away, through the fence. Sometimes they'll come over the fence right there,' he says, motioning to a spot a few yards away. " 'Hey,' I say, 'don't make me look stupid. Go a little further away.'"

While the immigrants enter through the fence, hundreds of Mexican shoppers flash their permits and go through the turnstile simply to shop in the several dozen stores that line Morley Street. Nearly everyone on the street and most of the retail clerks are Mexican or Mexican American. The rare bit of English is startling. One hears far more of that language on Avenida Obregón, on the Mexican side, where shills address every nonlocal in English: "Some more Mexican junk before you leave?" On the American side, only an occasional retailer enters the street to invite a shopper in, and then only in Spanish.

The stores are very much a mixed bag, though every one claims to be a *mayoreo menudeo,* a department store. A few, like Bracker's and the duty-free shop offering Rolex watches and Mont Blanc pens, cater to the middle and upper classes. The majority are aimed at the poor and the working classes, selling such items as boom boxes, twelve-dollar gold slingback shoes, and purple dresses, or a dozen earrings for six dollars.

Two little girls, their dark ponytails gathered in red and white ribbons, look longingly at a "life-size" Barbie-as-bride doll—actually a bit bigger than they are. The blurb on the box is in English: "You can dress Barbie up and share her dress too!" But the coupons another young black-haired girl is handing out are in Spanish, advertising four possible meal combinations at Golden Fried Chicken on Mariposa Street.

We stroll past the smiling New Yorker at the customs gate and enter Mexico.

There are some people who will tell you that Nogales, being a border town, is not Mexico. But even if you strolled across the frontier with eyes closed, stepping around the Indian women and children selling Chiclets on the sidewalk and ignoring the hawkers' shouts along Avenida Obregón ("Hey mister, why cross the street! I've got all the same junk over here!"), you'd know that wherever you were, it was no longer the United States.

You would be even more convinced if you raised your eyes to take in the side streets that run up and over the hill to the east of Obregón, or to the west, where a row of streaked pastel tin-and-cardboard shacks and two-story houses is tacked up like a Hollywood set at the bottom of a great, bare dirt hill. Or if you looked up to the top of that hill, where another row of even flimsier dwellings and makeshift fences, punctuated by oil drums and uncertain chunks of rusted cars and machinery, clings impossibly to the edge.

Along this gravity-defying perimeter, chickens and little girls scoot and dart only a few hundred feet from a ditch and fence climbing up and over that same hill. This barrier is clearly meant to contain something, like the ditches firefighters dig around raging forest fires. In this case it is the surging mass of cliff hangers, Chiclet sellers, hawkers, loafers, and just plain poor but striving folks on the other side.

Nogales is Mexico. In fact, like many border towns, Nogales is hyper-Mexican. Border towns cannot help but be self- and nation-conscious. They are themselves representations, billboards, moving pictures, flashing icons of whatever the nation is, or rather is from a particular geographic point of view.

We are in Elvira's, a gaily tiled restaurant just over the border, sipping Pacificos and watching an old man with a guitar move slowly from table to table, offering songs to American tourists and Mexican businessmen. He is surprised and delighted when we ask him for the *corrido,* or ballad, of Cananea.

A roving musician in Elvira's Restaurant, Nogales, Sonora

Father and daughter, Christmas Eve baptism, Nogales, Sonora

"That's real Sonoran," he says wistfully. His eyes are suddenly sad as he sings, in a thin but moving voice, of the great miners' strike of 1906, when the American owner, William Green, was invited by Mexican president Porfirio Díaz to bring American troops to Sonora. The corrido recounts the heroism and suffering of the miners. For the Mexicans it was in some ways the beginning of the Revolution, enshrined in song and story. For Americans, the event was one of many dark cross-border episodes conveniently forgotten in discussions of "illegal immigration."

We walk along the Mexican side of the fence through downtown Nogales and into a small church. In sharp contrast with the tourist trinketry outside, several dozen young Mexican couples are milling about happily with their infants gaily, sometimes fantastically, decked out for baptism. Maeve begins to photograph but is soon handed many other cameras: "Can you take a picture for us?"

A hundred yards away, we are back at the Morley Street crossing. Looking up the same hill we had watched from the American side, we see several dozen men and women entering through something like a gate monitored by some local entrepreneurs. It is the same opening we had observed from the other side.

The mood is casual, there and down on the street, where youths and workers pass into and out of the little coffee shops and bakeries. Two policemen drive up and park between the pickups, facing into the fence. The young men are not idle after all. Buckets and rags materialize from nowhere, and they set to work washing the police car while the officers stroll comfortably into the street, sucking tooth-picks and chatting amiably with the locals.

Two extended bursts of automatic gunfire shatter the moment, and dozens of would-be emigrants pour down the hill, dispersing into Mexico. Everyone is un-certain of the origin of the gunfire, and a crowd gathers at the bottom of the hill, peering up the dusty road that winds southeast through the hillside colonias. The police very reluctantly draw their pistols and take a dozen tentative steps up the road. No more gunfire is heard, and the police seem to conclude that there is no reason to venture farther into the maze.

Like the mariachi Fernando Sanchez, newspaper columnist and Democratic committeewoman Carmen Villa Prezelski long avoided visiting the land of her parents. She was not repelled by the chaos of the border; it was her mother's talk that had kept her away.

"My mother and her friends had stories about the Revolution. One woman had a store back in Mexico, and she would tell about a group of men who burst in and took it over. They shot her husband and beat her up. They tore the gold earrings out of her ears. Every time we heard about their experience there, it was a bad place, a dangerous place. It was a place to get away from. It might have colored our thinking about Mexico."

Carmen told me this as we waited in line to take our four-wheel-drive Suburban across the border into Sonora. We were retracing her path of some thirteen years earlier, when, at the age of thirty-seven, she first went beyond Nogales.

It was not that her own life in Tucson was not Mexican. In a way, that was the point. Her barrio childhood was fully enclosing. There were no missing pieces or unrealized fantasies. Perhaps nostalgia would develop later when she had lost that childhood Mexico and needed to seek it farther afield.

"I am the youngest of eight. Actually my mother had eleven babies, but only eight of us made it into adulthood. I was born in Tucson. Everyone else was born on the ranch. Ours had been the standard homestead of a hundred and sixty acres, mainly for cattle. We also grew a garden for the family. My father would plant beans that he could sell, and then he also worked for bigger ranchers: breaking horses, farm hand, ranch hand, or whatever, so that he could get cash.

"Economics made them leave their ranches. My own dad felt he had to make more money. And then the state closed the local school and wasn't providing any transportation. They had offered to rent a house for my mother and my brothers and sisters in Benson so that the kids could go to school there, but that meant breaking up the family, and my father didn't want that. So we moved into Tucson, to Barrio Millville, where I was born.

"During the war my father worked for the railroad, like a lot of Hispanic men. And when the war ended, the Anglo men were hired back and the Hispanic men were let go. Then he took a job at an ice plant, which was handy because it was right by our house. He worked for them for many years.

"Our house was adobe, so it stayed comfortable. But we expected to be hot, so we just didn't complain about it. Everybody else was the same way. I remember my sisters all shared one great big bedroom with room enough for three or four iron beds, and my brothers all slept out on a sleeping porch. My parents had a bedroom, part of which was partitioned off for me and completely taken up by my little bed!

"Mother fixed all kinds of food. She made *tortillas de harina*—flour tortillas— every day. And her tacos were her own. She would press a thin layer of ground meat into a tortilla and cook it like that so that the meat and tortilla would cook together and then add tomatoes, vinegar, oil, lettuce, cheese, and salsa over that. She still makes them. They're really very good. And no matter what was served as the main course of the dinner, it was not considered complete unless there were frijoles to be had at the end. Papa had this thing with frijoles. Sometimes he would have just a spoonful, but he had to have frijoles at the end of the meal.

"I remember most a really closely knit neighborhood, a feeling of total connection and safety. People respected each other's privacy, but there was a public life . . . a constant going back and forth. People gave each other things. If my father's garden had too much produce, as it often did, my sister and I would go around with our little red wagon and give the stuff away. We would be begging people to please take it, hoping that someone would take it all so we didn't have to go to any more houses!

"Of course, a neighborhood like that wouldn't let you alone, either. If a kid was told by any adult to do something or not to do something, there was no question that you were going to behave even though the person was not a member of your family. And it had its share of gossip. Life was so public, there wasn't much that went on that everybody didn't know about. A lot of it revolved around the church.

"My parents never had a checking account. They did everything with cash. After payday my mother would go downtown and pay all the bills—water, electric, telephone—and do any shopping she had, so I would go with her. In those days, my sister Aurelia worked as a cashier at the Cine Plata, a Spanish-language theater downtown. Mother didn't want her coming home at night alone on the bus, so she and I would go and watch the last feature at the theater and come home with Aurelia. The manager would always let us in for free."

Carmen laughed, remembering the cinema, but then she was commensurately sad.

"There is not much left of Millville now, and Barrio San Antonio, which is right next to it, is undergoing a new insult at the moment. Aviation Highway is being built—a road that nobody seems to want, but it's being built anyway—right through it. In fact, there was quite a controversy about it. You know, stories in the paper about Doña So-and-So, who had lived there for sixty years and raised her family there, and so on and so forth."

I was curious about Carmen's use, several times, of the word *Hispanic.*

"You're right," she answered. "We wouldn't have used that word then. You would have called yourself Mexican, and nobody would distinguish between Tucsonans and visiting Mexicans."

I told her of the young mariachi Anthony Sanchez's use of the word *white,* meaning "not him."

"Oh no," Carmen responded, "we Mexicans would not have considered ourselves 'not white' at that time. That was an outgrowth of the 1960s—Brown Power. I think we thought of ourselves as white in those days. If someone was very dark, we'd say *indianito,* and of course *guacho* was used for someone from the south or interior of Mexico. Most of the people I was with would have been from the northern tier of Mexico or trace their roots to that tier and then someone . . . less Indian . . . thought of southerners as country bumpkins—smaller, darker."

As Carmen explained all this, we were bumping through downtown Nogales, Sonora, her body uncharacteristically tense, drawn up straight behind the wheel. All around us swirled Mexico: Indianitos, guachos, and people as pale olive as Carmen herself. There were death-defying pushcart men, lanky, purple-booted vaqueros strolling in front of smoke-belching trucks, and of course gangs of ragged children dodging artfully through the choking traffic.

"I'm always struck by the number of people you see on the street here, especially children," Carmen continued. "The poverty always strikes me too, and I sometimes get very philosophical and think if my grandfather had decided to stop here instead of going all the way to Tucson, I might be here myself. So that always gets me thinking, how different my life is simply because someone decided to keep going another sixty-five miles.

"I did come here as a child." Carmen smiled as she successfully negotiated a particularly chaotic intersection and eased us through downtown traffic. "Not with my family but with my neighbors, for rum runs. It used to be that each occupant of a car could bring one bottle, so people would borrow a child to go with them. The more people in the car, the more liquor. But we would just drive across to the liquor shop and then back. It wasn't until I was thirty-seven years old that I really went into Mexico.

"I was asked to go with a group on a mission tour here in Sonora, to translate and help arrange things like accommodation and meals with some families. I finally said yes, but I was nervous. I thought, If I get into trouble, that's bad enough, but if I get thirty-two elderly tourists into trouble, that's even worse!

"But I had a very interesting experience right away in Tubutama, the village in the Altar Valley we're going to today. The church there is unusual. You walk in the door and you have to make an immediate left to see the altar, . . . and when I walked in and turned to look at the altar, I had this really funny feeling that I had been there before. I knew very well, of course, that I had not been. But that feeling helped me. I thought to myself that I hadn't been there before physically, but maybe culturally or spiritually I had been there.

"And the people of the place were wonderful. I had such a good time, in fact, that I kept coming back, and over the years I really got to know the people there. You see, we started hiring them to do things for the group tour, like Chata, who would fix a big picnic lunch. The town used the funds to either help with the church or for the schoolkids, and in the course of several years they were able to get a new school bus. Especially with a couple of them, I built up a relationship that was not at all part of the mission tour.

"I guess my experience made me want to know more about Mexico. I've always taken a good deal of pride in being an American, and I consider myself to be a fairly patriotic person. But I think that I needed to come to terms with the bi-culturalness of the person that I am. One can be a patriotic American but also learn more about the ultimate place of origin and that kind of thing."

I asked her if she thought of herself now as a Mexican, a Mexican American, or an American who happens to be of Mexican background.

"I'm sort of schizophrenic about that. I think there are times when I'm an American of Mexican heritage and other times when I'm Mexican American, and even times that I call myself Hispanic, especially in work-related situations, because that seems to be the terminology that's used in those settings."

We rattled over thirty or forty miles of rain-broken dirt roads, climbing, winding, and dropping through a set of low desert mountains. At last we entered the eastern end of the Altar Valley. A modest river meandered past the reed corrals of simple *ranchitos*. In one field a man guided a shallow-bladed scratch plow pulled by a horse and a mule. In other, grassy fields some cattle and horses wandered, apparently unbothered by the buzzards just beginning to gather above a dead colt.

We entered Tubutama via a loose sand road that, just before it rises into town, dips into a wash. The low section was flooded, but nobody gathered there seemed to mind. One young couple crouched in the water under a footbridge, happily scrubbing their toddler. They smiled and waved to us as we surged through about a foot of tan water and bumped up onto the dry road again. Within a few yards we had rolled into a surprisingly elegant town square graced by a gleaming white mission church, elaborately carved inside and out.

"That's the church I told you about." Carmen was relaxed and contented now. "We'll go in later, but first we'll go see Chata. She's the woman I told you about who makes meals for the mission groups we bring down. If I know her, she'll offer to make us some lunch."

Chata met Carmen at the door like a favorite niece and ushered us in out of the baking afternoon sun, down a cooling corridor of thick, green-washed adobe, and into the large, fan-cooled kitchen. True to Carmen's prediction, within minutes of our arrival Chata had placed before us plates of homemade *dorados* (fried tacos), shredded local goat-cheese, flavored rice, and frijoles (Carmen's father would have been happy). We ate with gusto, and Chata watched with pride. The two women leaned on the massive wooden table while Chata talked happily, filling Carmen in on all the local developments since her last visit. There had been a wedding and a variety of incidents involving the road-building crew staying in town and taking their hearty lunches every day here in Chata's kitchen. Carmen told Chata about her sons' adventures.

Chata herself, now seventy-three, had never married. Instead, following custom, she had stayed in her natal home to care for her aging and infirm mother. She had expanded that role into a career: cooking, sewing, ironing, and caring for the transient doctors, priests, and road workers who happened to be in Tubutama. She had done the same for Carmen on that first trip to Mexico thirteen years earlier.

After lunch, Carmen showed me through the simple house with proprietary affection: a series of large, airy rooms separated by curtains, almost cool in the midafternoon summer heat. For the cold winter nights there were several small fireplaces. Carmen remembered her many hours in these rooms, but the large, sepia-toned 1920 marriage photo of Chata's parents hanging heavily in the hall bespoke a longer past and implied a future when some nephew or niece would reclaim the patrimony after Chata herself had passed on.

"You see," Carmen told me as we drove away from the still-waving Chata, framed in her doorway, "when I first entered Chata's house, the old adobe, and the way she—the way everybody here was, so very warm and gracious, it immediately put me at ease. It was so much like walking into someone's house from the old Millville days, like entering our own house. This is going to sound funny, but I felt as if I were regressing into my childhood. That is what I felt. The business about the geography—whether it was Mexico or the United States—would have been secondary. I felt as if I were back in my childhood. It was like being in another time, not another place."

We left the village and drove out onto a straight dirt road through the empty desert. Trucks passed us every ten miles or so, usually brimming over with families, waving and laughing as they bounced by. Storms wove through the mountains, sending us spatters of warm drops but never real rain and finishing with a huge double rainbow arching over the desert. Looking back to the north, we could see the United States, where the sacred peak of the Tohono O'odham, Baboquivari, held the horizon, taking no notice of any human lines drawn through the rocks and sand below.

A thirteen-year-old girl at Mi Nueva Casa, Nogales, Sonora

Mi Nueva Casa

When we visited her, Jan Smith-Florez was the attorney general for Santa Cruz County, but she took a rather broad view of her job, and, like Carmen, she knew that houses create and contain worlds.

We had come to her office in Nogales, Arizona, to cross the border yet again, this time to visit not an old house but a new one, "Mi Nueva Casa," a refuge for the then famous "tunnel kids." They had become famous because the U.S. television show *20/20* had recently broadcast a report on these young denizens of the large sewer and drainage tunnels that link the subterranean worlds of the two Nogaleses. Their portrayal had been mainly sympathetic, giving something of a human face to the children whom circumstances had led into a life based mainly on scavenging, guiding would-be illegal immigrants through their passage, and mugging unsuspecting gringos on the U.S. side at an opening in the tunnel near a Kentucky Fried Chicken restaurant.

A forceful woman of about Carmen's age, Jan talked rapidly and enthusiastically as we climbed into our car.

"It all began in December of 1993. Concholla, the mayor of Nogales, Arizona, asked the governor to have the National Guard open their house to these kids for three nights or so over Christmas. So, after we returned from the holidays, Dennis Miller, the county manager, was in my office and said, 'You know, it's a real shame we only do that at Christmas.' I said, 'Okay, Dennis, I'll join you and we will do something about it together. I have some ideas.' I always have ideas. Don't you ever ask me for ideas, because I always have an idea! 'I have an idea about how we can do it.' So he said okay and we called a group of people to a meeting, and that's how it started.

"And then Justice Feldman made the mistake of coming here, and I told him at a meeting that we had this going but we needed funding. He said, 'How much?' and I said $50,000. He said okay, and this year we got $37,500 from the state supreme court—juvenile delinquency prevention or reduction funds. You see, the house over there reduces our delinquent population in Nogales, Arizona, so I think it is a very creative, legitimate, and necessary use of the money, especially since the Arizona Department of Youth Rehabilitation in Phoenix—that's where the kids get sent when they're picked up in the U.S.—don't have Spanish-speaking staff. When these kids go up there, we might as well leave the van running, because they're going to be back. They don't have a place for these kids. They don't do anything to rehabilitate them. There's nothing there for them, so we're trying to do something here for them."

We had crossed into Mexico, taken two rights, and returned on a parallel road to within a couple of hundred feet of the corrugated metal border wall. Mi Nueva Casa was actually an old adobe row house not unlike Chata's in Tubutama but of more modest proportions and in the midst of transformation. Jan burst in, friendly but all business, and we trailed behind, passing quickly through a small living room dominated by a large television, another small room with four computers arranged against the wall, and back into the kitchen, where the two Mexican housemothers, Lydia and Ramona, happily presided over the production of white bread and bologna sandwiches, making the best of what they hoped was a temporary absence of gas for the stove. There were only two children there, but others arrived as we talked. Jan also showed us the other side of the home, also divided into rooms, where she hoped some sleeping accommodations might eventually be provided. We settled down on the living room sofa to hear more of her plans.

"We try to limit ourselves to the children who live in the tunnel, simply because our facilities are limited. There are somewhere between seventy and a hundred kids living there, and I think we've provided services to about fifty of them in a year. Now we have something like thirty dropping in for meals or hanging out regularly. We have also begun to take in the younger kids, because we began to see a pattern. I was in here one day, and one of the kids from the tunnel—he's about twelve—was here, and he had his brothers. One was about nine and another about four. If they weren't here, they would have been in the tunnel, and we want to provide some intervention. That's really our goal and our purpose.

"The TV coverage was pretty good. They said some good things about the kids and the house. People in the States had only seen them as dangerous, paint-sniffing delinquents. The reality is that most of them are trying to provide an economic base for their households. They scavenge on the line, scavenge on the dump, get whatever they can anywhere they can get it. And they are not orphans. Almost every one has a father somewhere and a mother somewhere, and they may have younger siblings. We have a ten-year-old who was told when he was nine that he had to leave because his mother couldn't afford to feed him anymore, that he ate too much. We had one kid here we put in school. His parents came here to work in the factories, but they left their jobs for whatever reason, and the kid didn't want to leave. It's hard to make a thirteen-year-old do anything he doesn't want to do. But he's really a pretty good kid, and he had an aunt here, and she was willing to give him room and board. But she couldn't afford to pay for school, so we said, 'Fine, we'll pay for that.' So now he stays with his aunt and doesn't even come here.

"It's a bridge. We want to give them some skills and some way of making a living. We had a kind of apprenticeship program. There were a couple of cooks, a couple of bakeries. But then we had that big peso problem. But the bakers and the others didn't actually have to pay the kids. The kids just learned the trade, and the baker, or whatever, got an employee. We paid for the food and fed the kids. That's what we are trying to do, not just give a handout but a hand up.

"We try to do an evaluation on each kid when they first show up, to get an idea of their health." She motioned toward one of the children busy at his sandwich. "Just the fact that he's able to drink that clear water over there is an amazing thing. See, they were drinking out of that contaminated sewer, bathing in it. Strangely, they haven't shown up with a whole lot of health problems. I think it's going to be the long-term effects.

"I do think one little baby has fetal, not alcohol, but drug syndrome. The baby is only three months old. The mother is thirteen. She came out of the tunnel about six months ago because she was hemorrhaging, and we provided her with medical care. She was six months pregnant. We hooked her up with a couple who seemed like they wanted to adopt her and the baby. It was an okay place. They weren't misusing or abusing her, using her as a servant and that kind of thing. But then I found out she'd been coming back here. But she's just dropping in, and that's okay. We need to make sure that she's okay and that the baby's okay. I don't think she's on drugs now.

"Well, I was talking to the little mother the other day, and she was breastfeeding the baby. Nobody had bothered to tell her the social decorum of even covering your breasts. Not that you should be ashamed of it, but, you know, it's a privacy issue. And I told her how important it was to touch the child."

Jan clearly had the courage of her convictions.

"As a Christian," she declared, "I cannot just sit idly by. If there's a problem that I can be part of the solution to, then I need to be part of that solution. I keep seeing these kids recur in our juvenile system, and we are totally unable to deal with them over there. We're not doing a good job at all. They don't fit. I never want them to love the U.S. I want them to always know they're Mexicans and that their future is in Mexico, not in the U.S. We want to make them good Mexican citizens. We want to equip them to live in Mexican society."

That reformation was to begin with the house. Jan surveyed the room we were sitting in with something like grim determination.

"My idea, see, is I want this place to look like a house. When I was a child, I grew up very poor in east Texas and Arkansas, and I know how important it is. Number one, there's no excuse for dirtiness, and number two, I want this to be a pleasing sight when they come. So I, in my mind, envisioned how we're going to do it. See, this table is already damaged. Well, the company has got to replace it. We're going to make them replace it and give us undamaged goods. I'm sorry, I paid full price and they're not going to get by with that. We're going to get a table for the TV. I scavenged a lamp with a southwestern look. I would like to have a photo album right there on the table. What do you have in your homes? Pictures, right? Well, I want to have portraits of these kids and put them all around. I want to make this a home for them, and how do you identify your home? It has your pictures in it, your memorabilia."

But the house was clearly only the beginning. A living embodiment of the Protestant ethic, Jan wanted to reform the Mexican society she hoped the children would feel part of. The *maquiladoras*—factories built on the Mexican side of the border by international business interests—had already begun the transformation, though the results have been controversial. Even the low wages paid were a big draw not just for local but also for more distant populations, and many thousands had swelled the population of Nogales, Sonora, as they had the other big border towns. For many critics, these factories represent foreign oppression, exploitation, and dangerous pollution. For others, like Jan, they offer opportunity and growth.

"I have also served for years on, and am a founding member of, our Economic

Development Foundation. I'm a member because development is the solution. It will take twenty or thirty years, but we have got to start. The maquiladoras are by and large fine. They will do a lot for their employees, but they also demand a lot. They demand that they be there every day *on time,* and they don't put up with 'My tía in Tiajuana died. I have to go over there.' Uh-uh, no way. I mean, there are some ways in which they are anticulture, but I will tell you—just as I have told Mexicans—Mexico has got to decide. Do they want to be part of an industrialized nation or do they want to be part of a different culture? Frankly, their traditional culture . . . It's not that they're lazy, it's just that they don't necessarily feel the obligation to put in the consistent type of work. You know, get up every morning and get in to work by eight o'clock and produce whatever it is you've got to produce and do whatever it is you have to do and get two weeks off a year. They have to decide if they want that or if they don't.

"What they've got is the *patrón* system. If you are a boss, if you are an employer, you are the patrón, and you are responsible for your people. You help them if their kids get sick. You own them. Maybe not literally and legally, but you become responsible for that person, and it's the same thing as if they were serfs. They have tried to take that same system, that was agrarian in nature, and bring it into the office, into industry. I don't think it can be done. They never made that jump, and I don't know if any country that had that system has."

"I may be wrong," she said, "but if the peso continues to devalue, and the country gets more politically unstable, then I look for a revolution in the next two years if they don't get their act together. They are killing any middle class they had. And I will say, although I am Protestant and Republican, I will say that I have suspected that it is partly the fault of the patriarchal system that is perpetuated by the Catholic Church. I guess it is a trade-off. They have to decide. If they don't change, then fine, they can continue with their old ways. But then we are not going to put our money into Mexico. It is total stupidity to do so unless they are willing to make that trade-off. We will go to Namibia, we will go to Korea, we will go to wherever we need to go. Sitting, as I do, so close to Mexico, I am very interested in which choice they make."

If choices were to be made, I thought, it certainly was not going to be these kids making them. We stayed on after Jan left, talking with the four or five children there at the time, at least when they were not absorbed by video games on the computer or cartoons on the television. One of them, Linda, was a beautiful girl of thirteen. It was impossible to imagine her living in the tunnels. Her smiles were all sweet innocence, and though she may look older than her years, any such impression was dispelled when she ran back into the kitchen and re-emerged soaked and laughing, having ducked herself in the rain barrel to cool off. Two boys of about ten—one thin, one stocky—lolled about, exchanging Pepsis until one of them, his curiosity piqued, came over to inspect my videocamera. We played with it together until he had learned how to make it work, and then we went out into the street, where Pablito turned the camera on his friends, taking rather naturally to the role of director.

Later, in the kitchen, we talked with Lydia and Doña Ramona, who were still busy making bologna sandwiches. "What do you feed the children?" we asked.

"What we have on that day," she replied, happily launching into a *lista de platos*. "I like to make them eggs—*huevos rancheros*—and chicken. And, of course, I like to give them tortillas with all their meals. And when I can't cook, like today, I make them sandwiches, but I prefer to make them *carne asada* [grilled meat] with tortillas."

She paused to push back the hair from the eyes of a young boy.

"I have no children of my own. I adore these children." She looked around at her charges with great affection. She spoke of the thirteen-year-old with the infant. "A baby with a baby," she frowned, and then turned to Linda, who was sitting

Newly arrived boys at Mi Nueva Casa, Nogales, Sonora

at the table and enjoying the occasion. "You understand how that happened, don't you? You will be careful?" Linda nodded.

Some months later we received a newsletter from Mi Nueva Casa, penned by the ever-energetic Jan Smith-Florez. There were reports of declining delinquency among her clients but also news of the young teenaged mother. Mexican social services had taken her baby away, and she herself had been barred from the Casa for disruptive behavior. Sadder still was the closing note, telling of an event only weeks after our visit: "In memory of Francisco Gastelum, who at age fifteen died when he fell off a Southern Pacific Railroad box car he was riding in Tucson. . . . He was a regular client of Mi Nueva Casa. His death has greatly affected the other clients, who participated in the funeral and wake. The body was brought to MNC for a period of mourning." These, too, are the things that make a house a home.

Artist Anastacio "Tacho" León, Imuris, Sonora

art and quesadillas

A Tucson friend recalled a drive through Imuris in the early 1980s, when the road-bed was being widened to accommodate the new four-lane Internacional. A bulldozer, busy pushing back the stony earth and prickly-pear cactuses, had uprooted an entire *chapelito,* a roadside shrine most likely raised in recognition of answered prayers.

"There it was," my friend told me, "like a big concrete tumbleweed, just being rolled away with everything else."

Progress of that sort is not uniquely American. The new highway has riven Imuris, the steady stream of fast-moving trucks joining the more local traffic to form a dangerous river rushing between its two banks: the eastern and western halves of town. The old center lies west of the highway. In fact, it is easy to see how the changing road has several times altered the face of the town. The oldest route, here as everywhere, followed the banks of a river and passed through the old square—the *zócalo*—that forms the center of every colonial town. But if you come here seeking the picturesque on the historic mission trail, you will be disappointed. The mission church still faces the square, with its inevitable gazebo, but the square is quiet and the church is nondescript. It has no sculpted decoration on the outside, and the inside has been completely replastered.

Leading away to the northeast of the square is what was no doubt the next main street, now a packed row of dusty, mostly drab adobe boxes. Trucks full of produce bounce through the ruts, and gangs of children play in the street as their parents stretch out or sit in bits of shade outside their doorways. This aspect of life in the town is no longer visible to the outside world, which passes by on the four-lane highway.

That road has provided a new front for Imuris, embellished with a group of monumental concrete statues rising from the roadside just as one enters the town from the north. They depict the missionary Father Francisco Kino, a Yaqui deer dancer, a miner, and a woman. Kino did found a mission here, and there are definitely women in town, but Imuris is very far from Yaqui country. The name of the town is O'odham, but there is no other remnant of those people here. And there are no mines.

The statues represent broader cultural symbols, however, meant to define the road and the entire region through which it passes. The mines are to the east, over the mountains in Cananea, of corrido fame. As for the Yaqui dancer (his ankles wrapped with rattles and an entire deer's head on his head), he has become a general Indian icon for both Sonora and southern Arizona, like the Aztec warrior for all of Mexico. Both are safely exotic now that the larger society sees them as non-threatening fragments of their former selves.

But most travelers pause here for lunch rather than history. Many of them are truckers, whose rigs form a moving wall of exhaust-belching steel along the highway and, when their drivers stop for lunch, block the front of the many *taquerías* in town. Those establishments offer the usual fare but also, and most notably, the *quesadilla* for which the town is widely and justly famous: a soft local cheese melted in one folded or between two small grilled tortillas.

Another sort of art, however, has brought us back to Imuris this time: the religious pictures of Tacho León. We had first met Tacho farther south, in Magdalena de Kino. As he had for years, he had come to the fiesta of San Francisco not primarily as a pilgrim—though he certainly honored the saint—but to sell his creations.

When we first met him, Tacho was standing on a corner close by the church, his booth crammed with jewelry boxes and tin-framed, reverse-glass-painted *recuerdos*. These mementos of the pilgrimage are brought home to adorn homes and shrines. Even the bright afternoon sun could not wash out his colors, scintillating on a background of crushed tin foil, each picture with a teal green or deep scarlet script recuerdo and hot pink roses glowing around a black-and-white photo of the recumbent statue of San Francisco Xavier. With them on the table were even more elaborate images of the Virgin of Guadalupe. They began with the same paint and foil, but in place of a photo, the figure was assembled with carefully folded pink cloth robes and a cutout paper head. These finished products were displayed alongside other religious artifacts brought in by their owners for repair: recuerdos, plaster statues, wooden santos. When we met him, Tacho was busy clipping tin and dabbing glue, his deep, brown eyes intent on his work.

Within the booth a whole domestic world had taken shape, presided over by the artist's wife and younger sister. They sat, cleaning *cebollitas* (scallions) for the grill under a collection of tin birdcages—also for sale, some of them occupied by tiny, hopping finches. Having admired and purchased some recuerdos but no birds, we asked Tacho how he had come to learn his craft. By way of answer, he pulled out an English-language booklet on the fiesta published by an American folklorist.

"From my father," he said, smiling and pointing to the cover photo of an older man in a booth very like this one. "My family has done all this for generations. We catch the birds, make the cages, and the recuerdos too. If you stop in Imuris, come to my home and I will show you."

And so we came again to Imuris, this time to linger and explore the arts rather than simply to pause for quesadillas before speeding on to the north or south. We found accommodation in a roadside establishment which, though named for the owner, I was to christen—not without affection—the Box o' Flies Motel. Having deposited our belongings in our room, we mounted our pickup and bounced through town, down the main street with its teaming urban life, and in the space of one turn, into a suddenly rural neighborhood with vaqueros on horseback and straying chickens. Just beyond that the slow, brown Río Magdalena flowed past modest but fertile fields of vegetables along its eastern bank. We rolled over what appeared to be a fairly new concrete span just upstream from an old wooden slat bridge dangling by only half its rope supports.

The road then turned south again, an interior route and a world parallel to that of the highway. Here, rough desert and stiff buffelgrass were interrupted by occasional ranchitos and rural colonias whose houses often were put together like children's tree forts, made from every kind of scrap brick, wood, and tin. Even the more substantial homes seemed frozen in the act of construction, smeared here and there with gobs of cement and sheets of plastic tacked to substantial wooden window frames. It was impossible to say whether any one of them was being built, was under repair, or was falling apart. Possibly all three were true.

After several wrong turns and many pleasant inquiries, we succeeded in discovering Tacho's little home, just off the road in a rural barrio. Like many others, it seemed to be crumbling at one end even as it grew a new room at the other. But that probably mattered little, because Tacho and his family—like the three Mikes south of Tucson—seemed to prefer living outdoors. A variety of major appliances sat in the small fenced yard along with a plastic rocking horse being ridden by a shy toddler and, seated on stools and random lawn furniture, the other members of Tacho's extended household: wife, daughter, sister, brother, mother. Several massive cottonwoods provided shade from the late afternoon sun, and everyone seemed more than content to loll and chat, a pastime that did not need to be altered in any way to accommodate our arrival.

Tacho was, however, pleased to see that we had sought him out, and after leaping from his plastic stool, he found a wooden birdcage/trap to show us part of his trade that had been passed down in several Imuris families. Kneeling in the dust before the trap, he illustrated its operation by yanking on the string as would some unfortunate bird in taking the bait. He chortled with glee as the little wooden door came crashing down.

"Caught!"

He then showed us his studio: two overturned plastic milk crates, one to sit on and the other for his work. They were sensibly positioned under a large, shady tree on the side of the house.

"This is where I work," he told us, inviting us into the magic space. He then opened crates and dragged out his materials: rolls of aluminum foil, piles of scrap tin, brushes, and dozens of tiny vials, each partially filled with different colored crystals.

"These are my colors," he told us. "Now watch."

Crouching on the earth next to us, he tipped a few crystals into an old glass, added a clear medium, and swirled the mixture with tight flicks of the wrist. Then he held up the brilliant cobalt-blue liquid for our inspection, like a magician performing for a children's party.

"Mire, milagro! Look, a miracle!" He burst into laughter with shear excitement and, I could not help thinking, a proper respect for the subtle mysteries too often missed in more precious and jaded artistic milieus.

"You're the Mexican Picasso," we told him, to the appreciative laughter of all. We thanked him and made our way back across the river and highway.

The late summer light softened in the neighborhood behind our motel on the east side of the highway. This too, though only yards from the traffic, was a hidden and quiet rural world. The dirt road swarmed with boys armed for baseball and curious enough to show off a dozen or two words of English to the visiting Americans: "Where are you from?" "I play second base!"

Just down the road a teenaged boy was training a racehorse, holding a stick and making him trot in circles at the end of a short rope, kicking up swirls of dust in the darkening sky. He smiled broadly as we admired his form, but when we asked permission to photograph him, he quickly struck a serious, formal pose, standing still with nearly Victorian dignity.

Walking farther, we discovered a strange blue canvas tent pitched alongside a van in a vacant lot. A few excited boys and dogs scampered around it. "It's the cinema! The show is tonight!" another boy skidded through the dust on his bike to tell us.

We peeked in the tent and found the proprietor, a smiling, very European-looking woman with gray-green eyes and long, softly waved, light brown hair streaked with blond. Despite the lightness of her skin, her full, flowing skirt and gold-toothed smile suggested a gypsy, as did her trade. Her much darker husband was inside the van, arranging a pile of video cassettes. After chatting with her about their travels—they had come from the south, stopping for several days in each town—we asked what film they would be showing that night. She didn't know, so she shouted the question to her husband, who was by this time showering within. "*El Streetfighter!*" came the response, stressing the last syllable as it would be in Spanish, which she repeated pleasantly, adding that the screening would be at eight and that the admission was cinco pesos.

We had just enough time to stroll back to the highway and devour a small heap of delicious barbecued carne asada tacos before the show. While we ate, the van circulated through the neighborhood, blaring a message into the still evening air: "Vengan ver [Come and see] *El Streetfighter,*" followed by a bit of the sound track: excited dialogue and the whomp of cracking boards or skulls. We ate faster, full of anticipation for this "medieval scene," as Maeve put it: a remnant of the life of the rural carnival, now being blotted out by television, which has reached even the most remote corners of the country. As the first drops of evening rain began to fall, we walked through the darkening dirt streets to the cinema.

"Pase," the smiling gypsy told us as we paid our ten pesos, waving us grandly into the curtained world within. It was not a tent after all but simply a roofless square made of three high walls of canvas, with a large white sheet serving as the screen. The eight wooden-back benches were empty. Behind us was the one-room van, with the family dinner sputtering on the gas cooker outside and a thoroughly homey scene inside. An old-fashioned wedding photo hung on the wall over a blond toddler who played happily and noisily in a his pen while his sisters scampered by. The woman paused in the doorway to wave to her baby and then poured out a huge bowl of *chicharrones* for sale to her customers. The husband continued to advertise the film over his loudspeaker, and the drops of rain, still few but large now, began to raise a sweet smell from the dust beneath our feet. We could see the shuffling feet of a few curious boys and dogs outside the tent, but none entered.

By 8:15 the rain had begun to fall more earnestly, and it was clear that no one else was coming. We decided to leave. The husband, silent and deeply glum, was leaning against the van. His wife still sat at her post outside the opening of the tent. She smiled sweetly and reached into an apron pocket for our ten-peso note. "No, thank you," said Maeve, "we'll be back tomorrow."

After a fitful, fly-pestered night and Montezuma's revenge from those tasty tacos, we had a parting conversation with Raul, our hotelier, a chipper young man who himself lived in an apartment only slightly grander than our room with his wife and two young daughters. The youngest was a willful and pretty redhead of less than three, thoroughly aware of her beauty and already brandishing a gold bracelet and earrings.

"My mother built the place," Raul explained. "She is only fifty-three. She worked hard all her life, so we told her to take it easy. Now she travels: to Mexico City, Gaudalajara. We are five, three sons and two daughters, and we have a ranchito with some goats and chickens, but we all work at various jobs. I manage this place."

Maeve asked him about quesadillas. When she had first come down this way years ago, boys would come out into the road with buckets of them covered with cheesecloth, selling them one by one to passing motorists. Raul was happy to recall those days.

"Yeah, they used to do that alright, but they stopped it because it became too dangerous. My little brother was hit by a car right out there." He motioned toward the highway just in front of where we stood leaning against his motel sign. "The boys used to play in the road, too, while they were waiting for customers, and they would throw popcorn in the air to each other and try to catch it in their mouths. One boy threw the popcorn up in the air over the road, and my brother jumped out." He mimed the action, jumping in the dust with his face tilted back in the air. "And he was looking up and the car came and couldn't stop. It hit him, but he wasn't very hurt. He was very lucky."

I thought of *retablos,* the folk paintings on tin picturing such incidents in bold forms, with black script or printing beneath explaining the event and a floating figure of a saint, perhaps the patron of quesadillas, in the upper corner. He made no such religious allusions.

"They only sell them out of the buckets in the bus station now," he said.

"I lived in Tucson for five years," Raul continued. "It's much easier here. There, in Tucson, you have everything you need, but you've got to rush around. You're always driving from south to north to east. Here you've got everything just up the road in the center of town. But the electricity might go off for a few hours and you never know why. That's the trade-off."

"I *like* it here," he continued, smiling broadly. "I would like to get work in Nogales, Arizona. I can be there in a half hour, and the dollar is worth so much here now!"

In the meantime he was enjoying life in Imuris, which, we noted and he confirmed, was still famous everywhere in the Southwest and in Mexico for its quesadillas.

"The best," he told us, "are Doña María's, in the yellow house just across the road."

That was our last stop in Imuris this time, a crumbling yellow house outside, a fabulous, deep green adobe within. Several thousand business cards were set in huge plastic sheets that were cracking, buckling, and peeling off the walls of the small dining room. In between were religious pictures, family photos, and posters of Mexican movie stars.

Presiding over this world was the ancient Doña María herself. Tiny, with long white tresses neatly fixed in a bun set off by bright gold earrings not unlike the gypsy's, she circulated slowly through the two rooms in an immaculate, nearly diaphanous white housecoat and slippers. But she mostly stayed in the kitchen, sitting, as if on a throne, beside her Formica table, pile of mesquite logs, and blazing wood stove. Frijoles sputtered in the earthen pots while Doña María made her paper-thin quesadillas on the griddle. She was attended by two young women—one with a baby girl in her arms—who manned the stove and fed the customers.

We ate four of the delicate folded-over variety in the dining room, and then Maeve went into the kitchen and asked María how long she had been there by the side of the changing road.

"Ahora, mire!" Now, look! she nearly shouted, and she flashed her fingers, 10, 10, 10, 5. "Treinta y cinco!" Yet the world she had made there seemed so much

Doña María and her family outside their restaurant, Imuris, Sonora

older. Maeve asked if she might photograph her, and Doña María agreed, leading everyone out into the yard to a precise spot under a mesquite tree. She placed the young mother and her baby next to her and, once positioned, the three smiling faces suddenly became nearly solemn, like the young horse trainer's had been when posing for his portrait.

We complimented her on her quesadillas. Though thousands of customers had done the same before us, she beamed in gratitude, and with the dignity of a queen offering an exotic treasure, she peeled off a tortilla for Maeve, carefully chosen from the middle of the pile. "Vaya con Dios," she said, and off we went.

Josécito, an eight-month-old pilgrim, in Magdalena de Kino, Sonora

La Fiesta de San Francisco

An old Mexican woman enters the chapel wearing a kerchief and a housedress, her bony fingers clutching a big vinyl purse and two versions of her favorite devotion: El Santo Niño, a seated child wearing a large, floppy, plumed Renaissance hat. One is a recuerdo, perhaps fashioned by our friend Tacho León of Imuris. It is a tin-framed pane of glass painted yellow, green, and pink over crinkled foil, with a photo inset of El Niño. The other version of her devotion is a small plaster statue.

With age-stiffened grace she edges along the saint's recumbent wooden body, pausing first at the feet and then at the knees, body, and head to caress San Francisco with her own precious objects, suffusing her Niños with the saint's *poder espiritual y milagroso,* his miraculous spiritual power.

Her moment passes quickly, and others follow, some newcomers and many regulars. They approach the saint as if he were a newly deceased friend, their faces suffused with familial affection, even sorrow. They touch him, and many lift his wooden body from the back of the head to show, it is said, that they are not weighed down with sin. And they kiss him, then bless themselves in the Mexican fashion, finishing the gestured cross with a kiss blown softly into the fist.

I have taken a seat in the side chapel to watch the continuous stream of the faithful passing the saint, all come to Magdalena de Kino to see San Francisco on his feast day, the fourth of October. They are of all ages and both genders, and they often come in families. There are Mexicans of all shades and O'odham who have come down from Arizona in strength, the children in shorts and almost all of them in huge T-shirts.

Children, some dressed for the occasion, make their first visit to the saint. Two little sisters wearing *Pocahontas* T-shirts pray on their knees. A teenaged girl carries a bouquet of bright red carnations and hands it to the taciturn attendant to place with the older, wilting flowers lining the wall. Another *Pocahontas* fan around seven years old arrives. She is far more Indian-looking than the picture on her shirt, even with a huge barrette of balloons atop her head. Two little boys of around eight pray together, their hands clasped reverentially in classic prayer position: the picture of trained devotion. When they finish, they retrieve their shoeshine boxes, bless themselves, and scamper laughing into the sunlight. Back to work.

A young woman brings her little son to see the saint and then sits next to me. She lives in Hermosillo, she tells me, and has never come to the fiesta before. I ask her if the saint was good for illness, and she smiles, agreeing that he is but adding that she has brought the boy for a *manda,* his conception and birth a gift to be recognized. "San Francisco is very good," she says.

"Is it Francis of Assisi?" I ask, and she nods. "Or Xavier?"

"Xavier," she corrects herself and seems sure now. Her happy, spoiled little Guillermo is four years old and is most excited about the plastic bag of toys he is carrying, which he takes out to show me. There are two sets of Power Ranger masks and foot-long Power Ranger figures. With the aid of these objects his brother and he can simultaneously *be* and play with their own devotional Other—a more encompassing icon, I cannot help thinking, than the saint beyond, though certainly less enduring.

Or is it? I imagine a stratigraphy: deep layers, hundreds of years' worth, of

San Xaviers broken by narrow but thickly packed strata of Power Rangers, Pocahontases, Darth Vaders, and so on. The young mother might have been reading my thoughts,

"They see them on TV, and now they're even making piñatas of the Power Rangers," she exclaims in wonder and a little exasperation.

Every so often a photographer, his T-shirt advertising a jello-wrestling contest somewhere in the United States, pops his head into the chapel, looking for potential customers. And outside, the production and sale of images—human, fantastic, and divine—continues apace. Little Guillermo, like other middle-class pilgrim children, will have his picture taken, complete with sombrero, on a nearly life-sized wooden horse in the plaza. Meanwhile, the images of San Xavier, Our Lady, and many other holy figures are offered for sale in the many religious article shops surrounding the church.

We had arrived a few days before to find the town already caught up in a whirl of devotion and amusement. Streams of pilgrims were busily seeking not only cures and salvation but also tacos, Tecate beer, and music.

The town has recently been named for Padre Kino, the seventeenth-century Jesuit whose missions we have encountered all along the road and whose alleged bones lie under a glass dome across the plaza from the church. Other missions lie off the main route to the east and west, but this one is the Mexican counterpart of the mission at San Xavier del Bac, just south of Tucson. Both draw thousands of visitors throughout the year. But this one, located in a Mexican town rather than on an American Indian reservation, offers the carnivalesque exuberance of a fiesta on the saint's day. Not Jesuit San Francisco Xavier's day, in fact, though it is his effigy that lies on a dais in this church, just as another does at San Xavier del Bac. October 4 is the feast of St. Francis of Assisi, the patron of the Franciscans, who have run all the missions in the region since displacing the Jesuits in 1767.

This confusion hardly matters to the pilgrims, who are, after all, on their way to visit a corporeal San Francisco, the saint lying in the church, who has already answered many prayers. He it is who will receive their prayers for help and their thanks for miracles performed.

Outside the chapel, dozens of pilgrims were resting on the grass, picnicking and chatting in family groups. Among them was Pilar, a young Mexican American we had met in South Tucson. She was sitting on a blanket next to a much bigger woman, who turned out to be her sister, Elena. Pilar seemed less surprised to see us than we her, no doubt because she was, after all, closer to home.

"I love to come here," she told us, tossing her thick black hair over her shoulder. "I've been coming for the pilgrimage all my life. When we were kids, the whole family would walk down—at least sixteen people, the whole way from South Tucson. It would take us a week, so we'd leave on the twenty-seventh of September. The older ones would drive and relieve the walkers with water, food, and foot massages. Oh yeah, you'd need that 'cause your feet would hurt *sooo* much. And the older ones would bring lawn chairs in the truck too so that we could sit down for a rest. They would watch us young ones—the children—like we were a litter of puppies."

She laughed, and we asked her if she and her sister enjoyed the fiesta as children.

"Well," she answered, "we have never actually seen the fiesta, you know—all the food and the music. We would arrive and go to see San Francisco, and that was it. Then we would drive back home. Now people drive both ways. Nobody in my family walks anymore. My mother says, 'You quit way before we did!' and I guess that's true. But one reason is we didn't want the older people to worry anymore, or to put them in danger, because the old men always felt it was their job to watch out for the young people. I remember one old man who was supposed to be watching out for us. He got so tired that he fell asleep walking! So we didn't want to put them through it any longer."

Talking about this, her face—and that of her sister—had been almost solemn with concern, but now she was merry again. "But we still walk—my sister and me—many Sundays just down to the San Xavier Mission. It's only a few miles, but we have to be provided with soda, chips, *everything*. Then when we get there I call my husband and tell him to pick us up. 'We're lazy now,' I tell him. 'It's what we're used to.'

"Anyway, my little sister here couldn't make it back on foot if she tried. I remember, when I was a little girl, the first time we took her here. She was born premature just weeks before the pilgrimage, and my father carried her all the way down to Magdalena in a shoe box! She was that tiny. And he looked down at her and cried, out of guilt for how small she was, like maybe he shouldn't have taken her. But now he doesn't cry anymore, because she is so fat!"

They both laughed heartily as Pilar looks at her sister with great affection.

"It wasn't long after her shoe box days that she got wide. When we did the pilgrimage, she would sit down to rest, and then she couldn't get up. Once I had to stop a guy in a truck and ask him to help hoist my sister off a rock. 'She's too heavy to move,' I told him. He laughed and laughed, but he helped."

The two of them almost fell over laughing as they recalled all this, but then Pilar suddenly took on the mien of a frightened teenager as other memories surfaced.

"When we walked on the pilgrimage, we wouldn't all be together as the hours passed. We'd spread out. One night I was walking alone. I guess I had lost track of my parents and sisters. I came up to a house in the dark, and there were lights outside and a whole lot of people standing around. So I thought it was a 'welcome house,' where any pilgrim could stop for food and drink. That's what they do down there, and you have to accept the hospitality because that's how the people get their grace. You can't say no, because they're trying to do a good deed.

"So I walked up to the house, but when I got up to it I realized that there was a wake going on—that's why there were so many people—and the body was right there outside! I was terrified, and I ran and ran and ran, and when my parents finally found me, they couldn't get me to stop running. My father said, 'Oh my God, what's wrong with her—something's happened!' He was so upset that his heart began to beat badly, and he was so afraid and upset for whatever had happened to me that he got really sick."

Her sister added, "Another time on the pilgrimage we were alone together walking when we came upon this man just sitting in the wash. He was dressed head to toe in black, and when he saw us he smiled and said, 'Buenos días.' Just that. Then the next day, we were miles and miles away, but we came upon him again, still dressed all in black, and again he only said, 'Buenos días.' We were terrified, because we knew he was a ghost."

By late morning the receiving line for the saint is long, stretching out from his chapel and across the square. The most popular, not surprisingly, are versions of the saint inside the chapel. They range in size from a few inches to perhaps four feet long. All are robed in Franciscan brown, and the smaller ones usually are enclosed in tin-and-glass caskets, with their robes of cloth. The larger ones, fashioned of solid plaster, are often bought for communal rather than personal or household shrines. There are also images of the Virgin of Guadalupe—by far the most ubiquitous icon of Mexican Catholicism—and a variety of other popular saints and devotional figures: Jude, the Santo Niño, the Sacred Heart (the Jesuits came back), and even large ceramic piggy banks produced by the same technique and in the same factory as the saints. The sacred objects may be brought to the saint, taking advantage of the charisma of the place and occasion, like the Santo of the kerchiefed Mexican woman.

Where the row of shops ends, the temporary fiesta stalls begin, forming an enclosing tunnel of colors and smells: heavy chunks of sugary Mexican candies and caramels; bags and bins of every kind of root, herb, and seed for curing and strengthening frail bodies; and, of course, more mundane mementos like hats, T-shirts, toys, lipstick, combs, and hair-ribbons. Beyond are less official religious items, including images of saints and herbs joined in potent fetish bundles.

We wandered through this potpourri, sampling *cocteles de elote* (corn scraped off the cob and mixed with butter, lime juice, chile powder, and shaved Mexican cheese) and emerged finally into the open streets. Dark had fallen, and in the flood-lights the colors were even more intense and alive with movement. The wandering balloon sellers were now mountains of red, blue, and yellow floating among bark-ing blanket-salesmen and noisy shell-games. Of course, there was also more food, not only stands serving *elotes, tortas, churritos,* chips, and *exquisito* hotdogs but also slapped together shacks and open-air restaurants bathed in the irresistible aroma of searing *cebollitas* and mesquite-grilled beef.

Families of pilgrims ate what others cooked in open-air restaurant kitchens that could have been in their homes. We ate tacos and tamales in one homey spot, a domestic world that should have taken months in the making. There were re-frigerators and tables covered with green and blue plastic tablecloths and burdened with every kind of pot, pan, and cleaver. Perched overhead was a television. A mother and two daughters joked with one another as they flipped tortillas on the grill and whacked steak into taco-sized tidbits, glancing up now and again to catch up on their favorite soap opera.

Behind the town square was an entire amusement park populated by gangs of running children and a handful of hardy adults. There were the usual rides, like the octopus, with its spinning carloads of screaming children, but also something more idiosyncratically Mexican: a shooting gallery. Here, marksmen were rewarded not with Kewpie dolls but with a show: a bullseye sent a box of puppets into spastic, lurid, musical action. One gallery was named after Los Tigres del Norte (a popular

Under a food stand at the Fiesta de San Francisco, Magdalena de Kino

Mexican band) and contained a row of fully outfitted *norteño* musicians, including a lead singer wearing an automatic rifle slung over his shoulder. They all swayed to the music while, below, a puppet couple danced, the man's hands lifting his partner so that her wooden legs could sway freely with the movement.

Real bands—mariachi, norteño, trio, Sinaloense—played all around the center of town, in the streets, on the corners, or in pavilions. In one Tecate beer tent, a group moved a pale young vaquero from Chihuahua to a solo performance. His face, blissfully drunk, was just visible under a slouched black cowboy hat, and his nearly unbuttoned green silk shirt clung and billowed as he spun and kicked his boots to the sounds of a small band, whose mood was serious despite the gay red fringe swaying on their white shirts. An insistent saxophone, backed by the punctuated rhythm of a snare drum, urged on his slim, black-jeaned cowboy hips in tight circles.

In a moment the vaquero had pulled up a leather-vested buddy to dance with, or at least next to, him—an older, darker man with a thick, drooping mustache. His loose, thin limbs moved less frenetically but more easily, not unlike the dancing puppets in the Tigres del Norte box. Then a third man popped up, a stranger this time. He was middle-aged and fat and wore a plaid work shirt and dusty jeans, but with his hips swaying and one fist pumping the air, he was all macho grace, staking out a space on the dance floor in friendly challenge.

The young Chihuahuan took the fat man's hat, and he quickly returned the favor, leaving the two bare-headed vaqueros circling one another on the floor, each spinning the other's hat and beaming at the cheering crowd. But the fat man, though less showy, was steadier, and when the young one faltered, he snatched back his own hat and, pumping his fist in the air again, yelled "Viva Sonora!"

But the young vaquero did not seem to notice, and when the drums and staccato sax started again, he again took to the floor, crouching, spinning, and nodding with an imaginary partner. Now totally soaked in sweat, he grabbed a pretty, round waitress, pulling her into a manic embrace. She laughed with excitement, her face caught between desire and caution as he wheeled her around in a cross between a polka and a hip-lifting lambada. Striking a surprisingly graceful pose, she went along for the ride, finding a way to hold on to his slick silk shirt with carefully placed fingertips. The musicians picked up the tempo and his dance became wilder, pulling her nearly off her feet through stoop, lift, and spin until finally, as the music ended, she twirled away from him, back to the safety of the bar and her laughing girlfriends.

Then it was another song, and the dancing turned Mediterranean again—all male. The three men were up, gyrating their hips toward one another, the mustached "puppet" making slow, almost Caribbean moves. The musicians picked up the tempo, and the fat guy puffed but held up the honor of Sonora as the young Chihuahuito—his green shirt now soaking wet—kicked and stooped as if in a trance, his gold chains bouncing off a hairless chest.

We were returned to the world by a familiar phrase in English: "Where you from?" The standard question from a fellow American abroad. We recognize a compatriot by dress or language, and amid a sea of foreigners we think they are kin, that we have an inherent right to conversation that will only be welcomed.

This time the question came from a Native American dressed like many a southern Arizonan in jeans, cowboy boots, and a denim shirt. His deep brown eyes flickered with uncertainty above a tentative smile.

"I'm from Casa Grande," he added. "This is my first time down here. It's really something. I don't know anyone here. I could meet a lot of Indians but I don't want to hang out with them. I see enough Indians at home."

"Hey, do you know what this money is?" He showed us an old 1000 peso coin. "Is this a dollar? The guy who gave it to me told me it was the same as a dollar . . I paid for something in American money, and he owed me a dollar change, and he told me that this was the same as a dollar."

We told him that it was worth about thirty cents.

"So he cheated me," he said, more quizzical than angry, accepting the inevitable result of an exchange where he did not know the people, the language, or the rules.

We made our way back to the central square, where we saw a clutch of immense O'odham men. They had just come out of the side-chapel, where they had taken their own statue of San Francisco Xavier to be blessed by contact with the saint lying within. Their San Francisco was big, about as large as could be found outside a church. I had, in fact, seen the same statue earlier inside the main part of the church. It had been laid on a pew there, with an O'odham woman sitting in silent vigil alongside. Now outside, the saint was set on a kind of platform, reclining in open-eyed death and draped carefully in colorful cloth as if he were already back home in his village shrine.

We had met many O'odham for whom the pilgrimage was important. Once, bouncing over the dirt reservation road south of Tucson, we had accompanied a young O'odham who had been arrested for being in the wrong place at the wrong time. We were on our way to court, where he was about to be sentenced to a few months in prison. Staring out over the road, his round face suddenly broke into a beautiful smile. "We used to go this way on the pilgrimage to Magdalena," he said. "We would walk for four days, with a medicine man. It was beautiful." After a moment of silence, he asked, "Hey, do you think they'd let me out of jail for a few days so I could make the pilgrimage to Mexico?"

Here in Magdalena, the O'odham men stood around their saint with their characteristic deep reserve, speaking very little to one another and not at all to others. They seemed totally familiar with the moment, having come here like so many others and for so many years to the center of their cult, to see their saint, to recharge their own version. Yet, at the same time, they appeared totally ill at ease, out of place. They moved with a kind of awkwardness that is not at all characteris-

O'odham with their saint, Magdalena de Kino

tic of the Mexican, non-O'odham pilgrims. In different ways I had seen it all day as they drank their Pepsis in the makeshift cantinas or asked the price—always in English—of rubber combs or holy pictures.

The Mexicans enter every such scene with assurance. In the church, where San Xavier's statue is laid out as at a wake, men and women alike stroke, lift, and kiss their poor saint—his white face and black beard are reddened with lipstick—and bless themselves with balletic flicks of the wrist. Every move is easy, graceful, familiar. They can be slick, complacent, calm, or shaking with tears, but the Mexicans seem always sure-footed, as they perhaps always are in the presence of the dead.

The O'odham men stood around their statue, very much as if they did not know what came next. They were rooted in foreign ground, and they would not—perhaps could not—move. I admired the statue, and the compliment was simply acknowledged. But they were perhaps simply standing at the brink of the moment, their task achieved. They paused, looking in any and no direction, and finally, without a signal from anyone, the largest of them swept the wooden saint up into his arms and carried him, as one would a wounded friend, across the churchyard and down the darkening streets of Magdalena de Kino to the pickup truck or Bronco that would carry everyone back to another region of their ancient territory, now part of the United States.

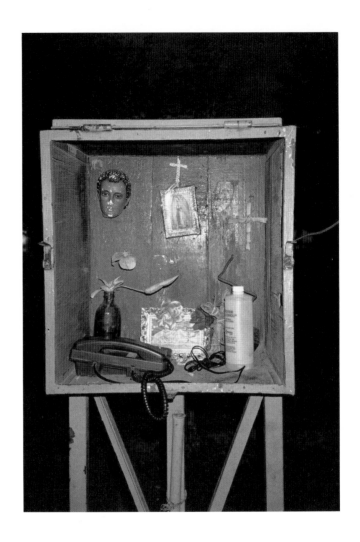

A taxi stand in Plaza Juárez, Magdalena de Kino

Magdalena off-season

First a full-arching rainbow lights the evening, one end finding the earth just next to a Farmacia Kodak sign. Then, impossibly, just above it, a second rainbow more faintly echoes the first.

It is 7:30, and gray and pink clouds are melting into the darkening sky over Plaza Juárez. This is the "secular" square of Magdalena de Kino, ringed by boot shops and groceries and home to strolling musicians, taxi drivers, and hotdog sellers.

Then the rains come.

We are watching the scene, staring out from beneath the arcade as the soft smell of dusty wind faintly tinged with carne asada and dog urine gives way to the heavy, earth-sweet, trashy stink of hard rain—rain hard enough that, after only twenty minutes, all the side streets leading out of the plaza are flooded and the high curbs have become embankments. But the curbs end abruptly, like everything constructed by human hands here, and I run, wade, and high-step through the flowing torrents back to the hotel on the edge of town to get the pickup. The streaks of lightning are almost anticlimactic.

All this and no fiesta, though there is something of a holiday mood.

I had driven back to the square thinking that the rain would have routed all and brought the evening to an early end. Not so. Here, as in the desert, the rains — *las aguas* — seem to elicit flowers.

At first, adults plod homeward or shopward, not acknowledging the rain. But when the heavens let loose, car after car skirts the plaza, letting off gaily dressed young women out for an evening rendezvous at the pharmacy. All the family cars seem to be driven by toddlers, who, perched on a parent's lap, peer out of the window, sometimes leaning into the rain. A hand-painted Volkswagen bug with cloud murals circles the square, passing a taxi with the church of Magdalena painted on its door. A bouncy blue pickup jolts up to the curb, and a young woman's leg emerges, its red shoe reaching the pavement. The driver, a sporty young man in shorts and a T-shirt displaying the Aztec calendar comes out the other side and strolls unperturbed through the downpour to the sidewalk. The woman adjusts her dress and mounts the steps of the farmacia as if they led to a Hollywood opening. While she's inside, the young man whips out an old rag from the truck cab and holds it briefly up to the edge of the farmacia roof, soaking up the gritty rain. He nimbly dabs his face and neck with it, and then runs the rag methodically around the back of the truck before remounting.

A female hound has been driven from a shop door by a couple of cheerfully callous teenaged girls, one of whom squirts water from a bottle in the mutt's face. Now the dog stands disconsolate but numb in the middle of the flowing road, the rain bouncing off her shivering brown body with terrific force.

Two other girls, one carrying a six-month-old baby already wearing earrings in her pierced ears, are pacing under the shelter of the awning, joking about going out into the rain the few feet to their car. One darts into the shop and emerges in a few moments with a plastic shopping bag and, giggling, fashions a hat for the baby. They put it on her head and run, screeching with laughter, into the rain.

Another Volkswagen beetle arrives and out steps a thin caballero in worn jeans, boots, and hat. Taking no notice of the rain, he wades to the rear, taking a baby stroller and diaper bag out of the trunk. Reaching inside the bag, he pulls out a wad of pesos. He is standing in his cowboy boots ankle deep in the swirling waters and it clearly doesn't mean a thing to him. He wades around to open the passenger door and sweeps up the baby with the one perfect movement of the naturally practiced Mexican father. Now the woman can carefully get out of the car, stretching her high-heeled shoes over the rushing torrent to the high curb.

Blue-shirted stock boys sporting badges advertising the farmacia's sale of the week, are constantly visited outside by their *novias,* all of whom stay inside their cars. The boys run out into the pouring rain and squint into the liquid dark at heavily mascaraed eyes blinking above the six inches of open car window. Everyone is cheerful and laughing about everything. This scene, like so many others here, seems choreographed.

The next morning is clear and hot again, and we visit the saint. There is no fiesta, but San Xavier is not off-duty and is receiving a steady stream of the faithful and hopeful. "Lotería," a vendor calls out softly to those entering the saint's chapel. At the exit the tinkling sound of a bell sounds ecclesiastical, as if rung for the consecration of the Host, but it is an ice cream man selling *paletas* (frozen fruit bars). Inside, a photo of a car wreck along with a description in handwritten Spanish gives thanks for the salvation of a Phoenix family. Fortune and misfortune.

As the pilgrims file by, I am struck by the grace and individuality in their movements and gestures. There is personal style in this as in so much else. Men and women vary in how much they touch the statue and where, but most striking is certainly the extreme tenderness with which some, mainly women, caress the polished hands, folding their fingers over the saint's. One woman stares lovingly down, lost in San Xavier's black eyes. Another woman, in her sixties, waddles up to his pallet and leaves a bag of coins at his feet, a tiny flower under his chin, and more lipstick kisses on his wooden cheeks.

We stroll along the shops that surround the church on all four sides of the plaza, where, along with the religious objects, toys and popular images are for sale. If not yet sacred, some of them are certainly well past profane, like portraits of Selena, the tejana singing star who was gunned down by her own fan-club president this year. Her beautiful full-lipped face and enticing breasts beckon from racks of T-shirts suspended from the covered passageway before several of the shops, next to racks of others emblazoned with Our Lady of Guadalupe or the Sacred Heart of Jesus. I am filming them when a friendly voice calls out from inside the shop.

"Pase," enter. The shop owner, a friendly man in his sixties, shows me his wares: T-shirts, dresses, and sandals. But he is less interested in selling something than in meeting and chatting with this foreigner who thinks his T-shirts worthy of video. I mention the Selena T-shirts, and he is pleased to see that I recognize her but is even happier that I know Luis Donaldo Colosio, whose portrait hangs inside the shop, "y su esposa," Diana Laura Rioja de Colosio.

It would be hard not to recognize the name and face of the assassinated presidential candidate. The town of Magdalena, and indeed the entire state of Sonora, seem plastered with every conceivable sort of word and image—bumper stickers, campaign posters, graffiti. Two huge black mourning bows still mark the entrance to the town, and the giant form of one has been cut into the foliage on the side of the hill to the west of town. Colosio had been born and raised in Magdalena, and now he is buried in the town cemetery, along with his wife, whom cancer had brought to his side only months after his murder.

I tell my new friend of our visit to the Colosio grave the day before, where we met a young family who, having greeted us, asked in heavily accented English, "Where are you from?" They told us that they were from San Luis, in Mexico

Delivering a statue to a shop, Magdalena de Kino

near Yuma, Arizona. The young father's people, however, were from Culiacán and Mazatlán, to which they were then on their way, with another ten hours of driving ahead of them. They had followed an emigrant path that had earlier led to California, where hard work and study had gotten Miguel through a CPA program. They joked about being friends with Governor Pete Wilson: "He loves the Mexicans—like Reagan and Bush!" They had stopped there in Magdalena specifically and solely to visit the grave of Colosio. Lupita, the mother, read out every plaque and testimonial for the benefit of her husband, Miguel, and two very young girls of perhaps four and six.

I asked what was responsible for the depth of their interest.

"It's like Kennedy's grave," Miguel said.

The comparison was interesting. The similarities were obvious, and the differences as well. Both lie now with their glamorous wives, attracting steady streams of visitors. But in Arlington the charisma of the martyred Kennedy is well contained, and the stately, simple grave occupies the moral high ground of a national military cemetery. Colosio's more familial new home, on the other hand, is in a local cemetery, one fenced grave site tightly wedged among hundreds, bordered by a rural slum.

Still, the pilgrims come, a steady trickle on any given day and crowds during the fiesta and, of course, the Day of the Dead. They seem, to some extent, a different crowd from those who visit the saint—better off on the whole, and often younger. There are few if any Indians, but many teenaged girls lean over the iron railing and look longingly at the photograph of the increasingly charismatic fallen leader. They adore him now as they would a slain movie star, as they do Selena.

My shopkeeper friend is very happy that we have visited the Colosios' graves. Hadn't he known the man himself as a young boy growing up there, playing in the plaza, coming into his shop? He too sees the connection to the Kennedys. Wasn't it all mafiosi, drugs, and corruption, as with those who killed the Kennedys?

The Day of the Dead in the Magdalena de Kino cemetery

"It was because he was going to reform the government," he tells me.

I tell him of songs I have heard in Tucson, ballads praising Colosio.

"Sí, los corridos!" he beams. "Y las poemas!" He asks for paper and, gently putting aside a Bible opened to Proverbs, carefully prints in capitals:

LA

    PRIMAVERA

LLEGÓ

    CON UN INVIERNO

QUE NOS CONGÉLO

EL ALMA

    JOSÉ BUENAVENTURA

The

    Spring

Came

    With a Winter

That froze

Our Soul

He has learned it by heart, he tells me. He then takes me outside to see its source: a poster in his shop window. On it, along with some words from Diana Laura, is the poem and a photo of Colosio's arm waving out a car window during a campaign visit to Hermosillo.

We turn toward the open square and look at the much larger than lifesize statue of Colosio that has materialized since our last visit a few months before.

"People come here now to Magdalena to see all three," he tells me, "San Francisco, Padre Kino, and Colosio."

True enough. The three representations triangulate the square, but the real bones of Kino are clearly seen by visitors as a curiosity, perhaps an archaeological wonder but not an object of devotion. They lean into the plastic window, gawking and pointing at the carefully excavated skeleton below, but there are no religious gestures. And though Colosio's cult is growing, his statue will not displace the saint's recumbent form inside the church. Closer than Goa, where the real saint reposes, Colosio's grave continues to gather plaques, flowers, and flags. There is no need to replace it with a statue, so the grave itself continues to be the central place for his devotees. But they may need a Colosio of their own to take home with them.

The manager of our hotel has one. Hers is a small color portrait photo with visionary words from a campaign speech set into a large leather map of Mexico. I admire the piece and ask where we might find one ourselves. Clearly delighted at our interest, she bustles into the office and reemerges with another copy of the photo.

"A small gift," she says, proudly offering the likeness. We accept the glossy little snapshot with thanks and head south.

A siesta alongside the Río Magdalena

lost pilgrims

For uncertain pilgrims like us there was no particular reason to make Magdalena de Kino the end of the voyage. All of Mexico lay beyond. In Santa Ana, just to the south, another fiesta was underway, a night of music and rides and joyous chaos. There was no saint, but there was a procession for a local beauty contest. Tightly wrapped in spangled gowns, local belles rolled by on the roofs of polished pick-ups, waving as their names were deliriously chanted by family members in the truck cabs and admirers lining the street.

The next morning there was a funeral. I was standing across the road from the church as the casket emerged. A man standing next to me had seen my video-camera. "That is important," he told me. "Film it, and follow them."

We did. The motley cortege led us to a parched, sun-bleached Mexican cemetery not far south of Santa Ana where the highway leaves the valley of the Río Magdalena and heads through the open desert. Its gate was guarded by placid white cement archangels: Gabriel and Michael. Inside the fence was the usual collection of graves and monuments. There were oblong piles of round stones, many of them overgrown by ragged grass and each marked by a white-washed, decaying wooden or simple black cast-iron cross. But there were also many edifices of concrete or even granite, some rather imposing.

As in all Mexican cemeteries, a white tombstone is just the canvas, the beginning of the aesthetic project. Ephemeral and substantial objects are added quickly or slowly to create an ever-evolving assemblage. One of the graves was an ambitious construction of potted plastic peonies set before a tile mosaic of the Virgin of Guadalupe encased in an arch of cement. The whole thing was topped by a large cement cross, bent forward over the grave as if melted by the sun. Nearby, perched on a simple but imposing flat tombstone, was a large, brilliant yellow, gaily lettered lard can. "Paraíso," it said, over a realistic rendering of a large pig. It held a bunch of green and white plants.

South again.

Beyond the cemetery, the natural and human landscape is spare and flat, a waveless sea of stony sand and scrub. Only a very few clusters of homes are numerous enough to enjoy an official name, the most intriguing of which is Benjamin Hill, who turned out to be a Sonoran revolutionary. Otherwise the monotonous desert is interrupted only by an occasional homestead, a few cattle, and *chapelitos,* the small enclosed shrines built by individuals for favors received and meant to accommodate the prayers of passing travelers. The travelers' other needs are met by roadside gas stations and restaurants, which appear every twenty miles or so.

We picked one of them, El Mesón Guadalajara, to stop for a late lunch in the hottest part of the afternoon.

Outside, everything seemed utterly still, all movement arrested by a relentless, uncaring sun beating through the dry desert air. A young girl of ten or eleven lounged under the portico, half sleeping in a metal chair.

Inside, the restaurant was cavernous and dark, the walls and ceiling hung with dozens of cowboy antiques. In the center of the room a large fan noisily beat the heavy air into hot gusts. There were no diners at the tables, but several women and children came in and went out or wandered in the shadows.

As we stood reading the placards advertising the menu, the *patrón* emerged from the shadows, almost impish and nearly energetic in shorts and sandals, a mop of black curls peeking out from under a red baseball cap. After commiserating with us about the impossible heat, he proceeded with brisk charm to recite a short *lista de platos,* including *machaca.* We were not particularly tempted by the idea of plat-ters of steaming beef in the heat, and by this time the dozens of flies that had found this oasis were visibly swarming. But his unrestrained enthusiasm for the dish was irresistible. Beaming through beads of sweat, he gestured like a French chef, "Con mucho ajo!" With much garlic! We both took his advice and waited with our cans of Tecate at a table beneath the fan.

Children now began to emerge from the shadows: a baby of about a year and an assortment of girls, every one of them with large, beautiful eyes, some brown, some gray or blue. The baby had blond hair and blue saucer eyes. A black-haired woman in her early forties circulated restlessly with one or another child.

To be thus surrounded by children, children tending children, is typically Mexican. These children, however, were American. That much became clear when the girl of about nine spoke very American English to her mother. But the mother, darkly Hispanic, spoke with a Latin American accent. We thought that they must have come in the van with the Texas plates parked outside. I offered a likely sce-nario: an American father (probably a blond Texan) and a Mexican mother, having taken their children down to see their grandmother somewhere in Sonora, were now on their way back to El Paso. I was right only about the American father.

The patrón, having proudly delivered the platters of machaca, tortillas, and a bowl of pickled jalapeños, gestured toward the woman with flashing black eyes. In caring but conspiratorial tones, he whispered that she was there with her eight

Exterior of a home in Las Viguitas near Imuris

children, that their car had broken down outside the restaurant the day before, and that they had all spent the night in the little chapelito near the restaurant.

"They're missionaries," he said, "y no tienen ni peso ni dolar," they haven't a peso nor a dollar.

He then returned his attention to our lunch, about which I was already feeling guilty.

"It's good, the machaca?" he asked rhetorically, every emphatic head nod accentuated by the bounce of black curls and baseball cap.

As soon as he had shuffled off, one of the girls—she was about nine with blue-gray eyes and hair in a neat brown plait hanging decorously behind—drifted dreamily to our table and told us her story.

They had been on their way to Guadalajara. "We are missionaries," she said simply, by way of an explanation for their movements.

"For which church?" we asked.

"It's called 'The Family,' but we work with everybody."

She went on to tell us of their misadventures, how the car had broken down, how some men had tried unsuccessfully to help fix it, and how the people at the restaurant had let them stay there and had given them a loaf of bread. They had been traveling with peanut butter, that definitively American food, so they had eaten that with the bread. Her father had gone to Nogales, Arizona, because he believed they would charge him too much to fix the car in this area. He was also arranging for them to stay in a hotel there in Nogales. They had spent the night sleeping on the ground in the little chapel, and it had been pretty bad.

The mother (from Chile, so the patrón had told us) walked with her arm around the nine-year-old, finding out what had passed between us. She came over to our table a few minutes later and, in answer to our questions, told us the same story in more detail.

She had eleven children, of whom eight were with her on this trip. The baby was about a year old, and the eldest was something like twelve. We noted, and she smiled shyly in agreement, that all were beautiful—*angelitos,* the patrón had called them.

The poor woman had been bitten on the breast in the night by some spider or insect in the chapelito and had a large, festering, burning wound.

"We are missionaries and we were on our way to Guadalajara. We had a job there and a place to live for a year. We've been there already two years. We drove from California. It was terribly hot.

"Maybe the Lord is telling us not to go to Guadalajara, because we had a lot of problems on this trip. Usually we don't, but this time . . ." She trailed off, looking a bit dispirited and certainly tired but calmer and less disconsolate than many would have under the circumstances. The girl piped in, "Two flat tires."

This was the big one, however, for apparently the transmission had given out and needed overhaul or replacement. God had let that happen right by the Mesón Guadalajara though, with many miles of exposed desert on either side.

But if the American husband trusted in God, he did not have the same faith in Mexicans. He had been dismayed by the good-hearted attempts of the passing truckers and had become convinced that no one in this country he had come to Christianize could fix a Toyota van. Rather than seek professional help forty or so miles south in the substantial city of Hermosillo, which is ringed by car repair shops, he had decided to hitchhike well over one hundred miles north to the border and find a "real" mechanic. He had left that morning, hoping to make the round trip in a day and return with a tow bar in hand.

God would then step in again, apparently, encouraging some passerby to offer to tow the crippled van and family of ten to Nogales.

Maeve had gone off with the mother to examine the bite and gave her both medicine and some money "por los niños," for the children. She accepted both gratefully.

"Yes, for the children. We live by donations. I don't want to see them suffer, but it is good for them to know that life is unpredictable and that they will be alright if something goes wrong, that things will work out. They have to learn not to have comfort all the time."

There were surprisingly few references to divinity in her comments. There was no doubt, at any rate, that she was a very caring mother, very affectionate with her children. Rubbing the medicine on her wound, she looked out toward the chapelito.

"We are not used to the desert, the animals. We were afraid."

Though kind, the patrón was less understanding. He came by every once in a while to assess our progress through the machaca and to comment, often with only an eye movement or other gesture, on the plight of his uninvited guests. He was not unsympathetic, but his genuine affection for the angelitos made him feel exasperated with the parents.

"Adults are one thing," he had told us. "If you want to go off like that, be missionaries, whatever, but all those children, to travel without money or provisions with those angelitos . . ."

The woman said, "Perhaps the Lord is telling us not to go to Guadalajara. We've heard a call to go to Russia. There's a big need for missionaries there. Maybe we will go there."

Several of the girls (there was only one boy in the group) had gathered around the table, all of them untroubled by their lot and apparently well acquainted with a level of discomfort, adversity, and uncertainty that would have long since driven most American children to or well past the brink of hysteria, or at least into a sullen, overtired crankiness. The three-year-old wandered by, prattling in English and Spanish. I petted the head of the four-year-old, who nearly purred while the mother continued to talk, openly and tentatively, like one who, if convinced of her faith, was unsure as to the meaning of the signs of the Infallible Will directing a van full of lives on this road to Mexico.

Several days later we turned back toward the United States ourselves, taking the Internacional north to Santa Ana but then turning west a few kilometers and into Santa Ana Viejo, the "old town." Boys were leading racehorses through the unpaved streets around the square, kicking up clouds of powdery yellow dust, while inside the church six women dressed in blue sang harmonic praises to Nuestra Señora.

From there we took the Mexican version of the Old Nogales Highway: a dirt road that runs north on the western side of the Río Magdalena. Like its counterpart in the United States, it is broken up, but by ravines and rocky hills rather than any highway. It was an easy enough trip as far as Magdalena, though, through modestly fertile farmland and cattle range. The road still serves tiny villages like San Lorenzo and Santa Marta, where we stopped for sodas at what appeared to be a small shop on the empty square. The outside wall of the shop was emblazoned with a tropically vibrant mural of the Virgin of Guadalupe. Inside, the few racks of chips, Pan Bimbo (Mexican Wonder Bread), and tinned vegetables shared the room with several armchairs and a huge bed, where about a half dozen small children bounced and played. Several adults chatted amiably over the din.

"Sí," they told us, laughing, "it is always like this here!" One of their number, a heavyset young man, asked where we were from. We told him.

"I'm from here, myself," he said, switching to English, "but I am living in Tucson now. I lived in California for fourteen years and moved to Tucson last year. It's good for me, because I can come down here to Santa Marta and see my family and friends. I coach their baseball team!"

We promised to return on our next trip, and then we set out again, north

A home market in Santa Marta, Sonora

Pilgrims' robes left at a roadside shrine near Santa Ana

through a sleepy landscape of wandering goats and sun-struck cows. After Magdalena the road was more difficult to find and rougher when we found it. Braving
several arroyos and patches of broken stone along the railroad tracks, we came
again into the river valley. Between expanses of rough earth were tiny hamlets
where whole families were washing laundry and themselves in a cement irrigation
trough. Just beyond lay Imuris and the promise of quesadillas with Doña María.

But we could not get the missionaries out of our minds. Missionaries without churches make uncertain pilgrims: no particular destination, no map, and only
their own stories to guide them. In some ways they were like any Americans and
like not a few we had met along the road, self-exiled on the edge of the desert,
looking for a place they might not recognize when they found it. Everywhere lay
a potential Holy Land. But this time they had gone too far. Too far into the desert.
Too far into Mexico.

Perhaps the desert chapelito in which they had found such uncertain shelter
was an unforeseen station on their pilgrimage route. And ours. Had they recognized it as such? Had we?

We remembered the photo of the assassinated Colosio given to us by the
hotel manager in Magdalena and decided to pay another visit to our artist friend,
Tacho León.

Tacho was sitting, as usual, with his neighbors and family on an assortment of
half-chairs and plastic crates in the shade of the graceful cottonwood. He bounced
up to greet us and, dragging a couple of broken lawn chairs out of the house, bade
us join them. We did, and Maeve pulled out the little color photo of the fallen hero.

An old woman took it from our hands and, delicately touching the portrait,
blessed herself. She then passed it reverently to the others, each of whom wondered sadly at the radiant campaign face of Don Luis Donaldo.

Tacho took the photo off to his "studio" and happily set about his work. He pried open one of his colorful recuerdos, and out came the black-and-white portrait of the recumbent San Francisco Xavier and in went the glossy Kodak of the new saint.

Tacho smiled proudly and rose to hand us the new icon.

"There have already been many miracles," he said.

about the author and photographer

Lawrence J. Taylor is a writer and a professor of anthropology at Lafayette College in Easton, Pennsylvania. A native New Yorker, he has lived and taught in Ireland and France, and has conducted fieldwork in Ireland, the Bahamas, and several parts of Europe and America. He is the author of several dozen articles on cultural and historical topics ranging from fishing to the political uses of death and of two books: *Dutchmen on the Bay* and *Occasions of Faith: An Anthropology of Irish Catholics.*

Maeve Hickey is an artist whose work in various media has been shown in solo exhibitions in New York, London, Rome, and other cities. Her work is represented in North American and European collections, and she has been a guest artist in Berkeley, Dublin, and Paris.

Hickey and Taylor are at work on collaborative exhibitions and another book of photos and essays on the U.S.–Mexico border.

Library of Congress Cataloging-in-Publication Data

Taylor, Lawrence J., 1949–

The road to Mexico / text by Lawrence J. Taylor ;
photographs by Maeve Hickey.

p.   cm. — (The Southwest Center series)

ISBN 0-8165-1723-1 (cloth : alk. paper). —

ISBN 0-8165-1725-8 (pbk. : alk. paper)

1. Southwest, New—Description and travel.

2. Southwest, New—Pictorial works.

3. Roads—Southwest, New.   4. Southwest,
New—Social life and customs.   I. Hickey, Maeve.

II. Title.   III. Series.

F787.T39   1997

338'.04'092—dc21

[917.904'33]   97-4578

CIP